Gran
Prefaces to Shakespeare

ROMEO
AND JULIET

Foreword by
Richard Eyre

NATIONAL

NICK HERN BOOKS

First published in this collected paperback edition in 1993 jointly by
Nick Hern Books Limited, 14 Larden Road, London W3 7ST
and the Royal National Theatre, London,
by arrangement with Batsford.

Preface to Romeo and Juliet. Originally published in 1930

Set in 10/11 Baskerville by Pure Tech Corporation, Pondicherry
(India)
Printed in Australia by
Australian Print Group

A CIP catalogue record for this book is available from the British
Library

ISBN 1 85459 111 8

Shakespeare Alive!

The history of the theatre in England in this century can be told largely through the lives and work of two men: George Bernard Shaw and Harley Granville Barker, a triple-barrelled cadence of names that resonates like the ruffling of the pages of a large book in a silent public library. One was a brilliant polemicist who dealt with certainties and assertions and sometimes, but not often enough, breathed life into his sermons; the other a committed sceptic who started from the premise that the only thing certain about human behaviour was that nothing was certain. Both, however, possessed a passionate certainty about the importance of the theatre and the need to revise its form, its content, and the way that it was managed. Shaw was a playwright, critic and pamphleteer, Barker a playwright, director and actor.

The Voysey Inheritance is, at least in my opinion, Granville Barker's best play: a complex web of family relationships, a fervent but never unambiguous indictment of a world dominated by the mutually dependent obsessions of greed, class, and self-deception. It's also a virtuoso display of stagecraft: the writer showing that as director he can handle twelve speaking characters on stage at one time, and that as actor he can deal with the most ambitious and unexpected modulations of thought and feeling. The 'inheritance' of the Voyseys is a legacy of debt, bad faith, and bitter family dissension. Edward's father has, shortly before his death, revealed that he has been cheating the family firm of solicitors for many years, as his father had for many years before that. Towards the end of the play Edward Voysey, the youngest son, confronts the woman he loves:

> EDWARD. Why wouldn't he own the truth to me about himself?
>
> BEATRICE. Perhaps he took care not to know it. Would you have understood?
>
> EDWARD. Perhaps not. But I loved him.
>
> BEATRICE. That would silence a bench of judges.

Shaw would have used the story to moralise and polemicise. He might have had the son hate the father; he might have had him forgive him; he might have had him indict him as a paradigm of capitalism; he would never have said he loved him.

Everybody needs a father, or, failing that, a father-figure. He may be a teacher, a prophet, a boss, a priest perhaps, a political leader, a friend, or, sometimes, if you are very lucky, the real one. If you can't find a father you must invent him. In some ways, not altogether trivial, Granville Barker is something of a father-figure for me. He's a writer whom I admire more than any twentieth-century English writer before the sixties – Chekhov with an English accent; he's the first modern British director; he's the real founder of the National Theatre and, in his *Prefaces*, he's a man who, alone amongst Shakespearean commentators before Jan Kott, believed in the power of Shakespeare on stage.

There was a myth that Granville Barker was the natural son of Shaw. He was certainly someone whom Shaw could, in his awkward way, cherish and admire, educate and castigate. When Barker fell wildly in love ('in the Italian manner' as Shaw said) with Helen Huntington, an American millionairess, he married her, acquired a hyphen in his surname, moved first to Devon to play the part of a country squire, and then to France to a life of seclusion. Shaw thought that he had buried himself alive and could never reconcile himself to the loss. It was, as his biographer

Hesketh Pearson said: 'The only important matter about which he asked me to be reticent.'

After directing many of Shaw's plays for many years, acting many of his best roles (written by Shaw with Barker in mind), dreaming and planning together the birth of a National Theatre, not to mention writing, directing, and acting in his own plays while managing his own company at the Royal Court, Barker withdrew from the theatre, and for twenty years there was silence between the two men. Only on the occasion of the death of Shaw's wife did they communicate by letters. 'I did not know I could be so moved by anything,' wrote Shaw to him.

Out of this self-exile came one major work, slowly assembled over many years: *The Prefaces to Shakespeare*. With a few exceptions (Auden on *Othello*, Barbara Everett on *Hamlet*, Jan Kott on *The Tempest*) it's the only critical work about Shakespeare that's made any impact on me, apart, that is, from my father's view of Shakespeare, which was brief and brutal: 'It's absolute balls.'

As much as we need a good father, we need a good teacher. Mine, improbably perhaps, was Kingsley Amis. He'd arrived, somewhat diffidently, at Cambridge at the same time as I did. The depth of my ignorance of English literature corresponded almost exactly to his dislike of the theatre. Nevertheless, he made me see Shakespeare with a mind uncontaminated by the views of academics, whom he would never have described as his fellows and whose views he regarded as, well, academic. I would write essays marinated in the opinions of Spurgeon, Wilson Knight, Dover Wilson and a large cast of critical supernumeraries. He would gently, but courteously, cast aside my essay about, say, *Twelfth Night*: 'But what do *you* think of this play? Do you think it's any good?' 'Well ... er ... it's Shakespeare.' 'Yes, but is

it any *good*? I mean as a *play*. It says it's a comedy. Fine.
But does it have any decent jokes?'

I took this for irreverence, heresy even. Over the years,
however, I've come to regard this as good teaching, or,
closely allied, good direction. It's asking the right questions,
unintimidated by reputation, by tradition, by received
opinion, or by critical orthodoxy. This was shocking, but
healthy, for a young and impressionable man ripe to
become a fundamentalist in matters of literary taste and
ready to revere F. R. Leavis as the Ayatollah of 'Cambridge
English'. What you have is yourself and the text, only that.
That's the lesson of Granville Barker: 'We have the text to
guide us, half a dozen stage directions, and that is all. I
abide by the text and the demands of the text and beyond
that I claim freedom.' I can't imagine a more useful and
more enduring dictum.

The Prefaces have a practical aim: 'I want to see
Shakespeare made fully effective on the English stage.
That is the best sort of help I can lend.' What Granville
Barker wrote is a primer for directors and actors working
on the plays of Shakespeare. There is lamentably little
useful literature about the making of theatre, even though
there is an indigestible glut of memoirs and biographies,
largely concerned with events that have taken place *after*
the curtain has fallen. If I was asked by a visiting Martian
to recommend books which would help him, her or it to
make theatre in the manner of the European I could only
offer four books: Stanislavsky on *The Art of the Stage*, John
Willett's *Brecht on Theatre*, Peter Brook's *The Empty Space*,
and *The Prefaces to Shakespeare*.

Stanislavsky offers a pseudo-scientific dissection of the
art of acting which is, in some respects, like reading
Freud on the mechanism of the joke: earnest, well-
meaning, but devoid of the indispensable ingredient
of its subject matter: humour. Stanislavsky's great

contribution was to demand that actors hold the mirror up to nature, that they take their craft as seriously as the writers they served, and to provide some sort of formal discipline within which both aims could be realised.

Brecht provided a manifesto that was a political and aesthetic response to the baroque encrustations of the scenery-laden, star-dominated, archaic boulevard theatre of Germany in the twenties. Although much of what he wrote as theory is an unpalatable mix of political ideology and artistic instruction, it is his theatrical instinct that prevails. He asserts, he insists, he browbeats. He demands that the stage, like society, must be re-examined, reformed, that the audience's habits mustn't be satisfied, they must be changed, but just when he is about to nail his 13 Articles to the church door he drops the voice of the zealot: 'The stage is not a hothouse or a zoological museum full of stuffed animals. It must be peopled with live, three-dimensional self-contradictory people with their passions, unconsidered utterances and actions.' In all art forms, he says, the guardians of orthodoxy will assert that there are eternal and immutable laws that you ignore at your peril, but in the theatre there is only one inflexible rule: 'The proof of the pudding is in the eating.' Brecht teaches us to ask the question: what goes on in a theatre?

Brook takes that question even further: what *is* theatre? It's a philosophical, but eminently practical, question that Brook has been asking for over 30 years and which has taken him to the African desert, a quarry in Iran, and an abandoned music hall in Paris. 'I take an empty space and call it a bare stage. A man walks across this empty space while someone else is watching him, and that is all that is needed for an act of theatre to be engaged.' For all his apparent concern with metaphyics, there is no more practical man of the theatre than Brook.

I was once at a seminar where someone asked him what was the job of the director. 'To get the actors on and off stage,' he said. Like Brecht, like Stanislavsky, like Granville Barker, Brook argues that for the theatre to be expressive it must be, above all, simple and unaffected: a distillation of language, of gesture, of action, of design, where meaning is the essence. The meaning must be felt as much as understood. 'They don't have to understand with their ears,' says Granville Barker, 'just with their guts.'

Brecht did not acknowledge a debt to Granville Barker. Perhaps he was not aware of one, but it seems to me that Barker's Shakespeare productions were the direct antecedents of Brecht's work. He certainly knew enough about English theatre to know that he was on to a good thing adapting *The Beggar's Opera*, *The Recruiting Officer* and *Coriolanus*. Brecht has been lauded for destroying illusionism; Granville Barker has been unhymned. He aimed at re-establishing the relationship between actor and audience that had existed in Shakespeare's theatre – and this at a time when the prevailing style of Shakespearean production involved *not* stopping short of having live sheep in *As You Like It*. He abolished footlights and the proscenium arch, building out an apron over the orchestra pit which Shaw said 'apparently trebled the spaciousness of the stage. . . . To the imagination it looks as if he had invented a new heaven and a new earth.'

His response to staging Shakespeare was not to look for a synthetic Elizabethanism. 'We shall not save our souls by being Elizabethan.' To recreate the Globe would, he knew, be aesthetic anasthaesia, involving the audience in an insincere conspiracy to pretend that they were willing collaborators in a vain effort to turn the clock back. His answers to staging Shakespeare were similar to Brecht's for *his* plays and, in some senses, to

Chekhov's for his. He wanted scenery not to decorate and be literal, but to be expressive and metaphorical, and at the same time, in apparent contradiction, to be specific and be real, while being minimal and iconographic: the cart in *Mother Courage*, the nursery in *The Cherry Orchard*, the dining table in *The Voysey Inheritance*. 'To create a new hieroglyphic language of scenery. That, in a phrase, is the problem. If the designer finds himself competing with the actors, the sole interpreters Shakespeare has licensed, then it is he that is the intruder and must retire.'

In *The Prefaces* Granville Barker argues for a fluency of staging unbroken by scene changes. Likewise the verse should be spoken fast. 'Be swift, be swift, be not poetical,' he wrote on the dressing-room mirror of Cathleen Nesbitt when she played Perdita. Within the speed, however, detailed reality. *Meaning* above all.

It is the director's task, with the actors, to illuminate the meanings of a play: its vocabulary, its syntax, and its philosophy. The director has to ask what each scene is revealing about the characters and their actions: what story is each scene telling us? In *The Prefaces* Granville Barker exhumes, examines and explains the lost stagecraft of Shakespeare line by line, scene by scene, play by play.

Directing Shakespeare is a matter of understanding the meaning of a scene and staging it in the light of that knowledge. Easier said than done, but it's at the heart of the business of directing any play, and directing Shakespeare is merely directing writ large. Beyond that, as David Mamet has observed, 'choice of actions and adverbs constitute the craft of directing'. Get up from that chair and walk across the room. Slowly.

With Shakespeare as with any other playwright the director's job is to make the play live, now, in the present tense. 'Spontaneous enjoyment is the life of the theatre,' says Granville Barker in his Preface to *Love's Labour's Lost*. To receive a review, as Granville Barker did, headed *SHAKESPEARE ALIVE!* is the most, but should be the least, that a director must hope for.

I regard Granville Barker not only as the first modern English director but as the most influential. Curiously, partly as a result of his early withdrawal from the theatre, partly because his *Prefaces* have been out of print for many years, and partly because of his own self-effacement, he has been unjustly ignored both in the theatre and in the academic world, where the codification of their 'systems' has resulted in the canonisation of Brecht and Stanislavsky. I hope the re-publication of *The Prefaces* will right the balance. Granville Barker himself always thought of them as his permanent legacy to the theatre.

My sense of filial identification is not entirely a professional one. When I directed *The Voysey Inheritance* I wanted a photograph of the author on the poster. A number of people protested that it was the height, or depth, of vanity and self-aggrandisement to put my own photograph on the poster. I was astonished, I was bewildered, but I was not unflattered. I still can't see the resemblance, but it's not through lack of trying.

Two years ago the Royal National Theatre was presented with a wonderful bronze bust of Granville Barker by Katherine Scott (the wife, incidentally, of the Antarctic hero). For a while it sat on the windowsill of my office like a benign household god. Then it was installed on a bracket in the foyer opposite a bust of Olivier, the two men eyeing each other in wary mutual regard. A few months later it was stolen; an act of homage perhaps. I miss him.

Richard Eyre

Introduction

We have still much to learn about Shakespeare the playwright. Strange that it should be so, after three centuries of commentary and performance, but explicable. For the Procrustean methods of a changed theatre deformed the plays, and put the art of them to confusion; and scholars, with this much excuse, have been apt to divorce their Shakespeare from the theatre altogether, to think him a poet whose use of the stage was quite incidental, whose glory had small relation to it, for whose lapses it was to blame.

The Study and the Stage

THIS much is to be said for Garrick and his predecessors and successors in the practice of reshaping Shakespeare's work to the theatre of their time. The essence of it was living drama to them, and they meant to keep it alive for their public. They wanted to avoid whatever would provoke question and so check that spontaneity of response upon which acted drama depends. Garrick saw the plays, with their lack of 'art', through the spectacles of contemporary culture; and the bare Elizabethan stage, if it met his mind's eye at all, doubtless as a barbarous makeshift. Shakespeare was for him a problem; he tackled it, from our point of view, misguidedly and with an overplus of enthusiasm. His was a positive world; too near in time, moreover, as well as too opposed in taste to Shakespeare's to treat it perspectively. The romantic movement might have brought a more concordant outlook. But by then the scholars were off their own way; while the theatre began to think of its Shakespeare from the point of view of the picturesque, and, later, in terms of upholstery. Nineteenth-century drama developed along the lines of realistic illusion, and the staging of Shakespeare was further subdued to this, with inevitably disastrous effect on the speaking of his verse; there was less perversion of text perhaps, but actually more wrenching of the construction of the plays for the convenience of the stage carpenter. The public appetite for this sort of thing having been gorged, producers then turned to newer—and older—contrivances, leaving 're-alism' (so called) to the modern comedy that had fathered it. Amid much vaporous theorizing—but let us humbly own how hard it is not to write nonsense about art, which seems ever pleading to be enjoyed and not written about at all—the surprising discovery had been made that varieties of stagecraft and stage were not historical accidents but artistic obligations, that Greek drama belonged in a Greek theatre, that Elizabethan plays, therefore, would, presumably, do best upon an Elizabethan stage, that there was nothing sacrosanct about scenery, footlights, drop-curtain or any of their belongings. This brings us to the present situation.

There are few enough Greek theatres in which Greek tragedy can be played; few enough people want to see it, and they will applaud it encouragingly however it is done. Some acknowledgement is due to the altruism of the doers! Shakespeare is another matter. The English theatre, doubtful of its destiny, of necessity venal, opening its doors to all comers, seems yet, as by some instinct, to seek renewal of strength in him. An actor, unless success has made him cynical, or his talent be merely trivial, may take some pride in the hall mark of Shakespearean achievement. So may a manager if he thinks he can afford it. The public (or their spokesmen) seem to consider Shakespeare and his genius a sort of national

property, which, truly, they do nothing to conserve, but
in which they have moral rights not lightly to be flouted.
The production of the plays is thus still apt to be marked
by a timid respect for 'the usual thing'; their acting is
crippled by pseudo-traditions, which are inert because
they are not Shakespearean at all. They are the accu-
mulation of two centuries of progressive misconception
and distortion of his playwright's art. On the other hand,
England has been spared production of Shakespeare
according to this or that even more irrelevant theory of
presentationalism, symbolism, constructivism or what
not. There is the breach in the wall of 'realism', but we
have not yet made up our minds to pass through, taking
our Shakespeare with us.

Incidentally, we owe the beginning of the breach to
Mr William Poel, who, with fanatical courage, when
'realism' was at the tottering height of its triumph in the
later revivals of Sir Henry Irving, and the yet more richly
upholstered revelations of Sir Herbert Tree, thrust the
Elizabethan stage in all its apparent eccentricity upon
our unwilling notice.[1] Mr Poel shook complacency. He
could not expect to do much more; for he was a logical
reformer. He showed us the Elizabethan stage, with
Antony and Cleopatra, Troilus and Cressida, in their
ruffs and farthingales as for Shakespeare's audiences they
lived. Q.E.D. There, however, as far as the popular
theatre was concerned, the matter seemed to rest for
twenty years or so. But it was just such a demonstration
that was needed; anything less drastic and provocative
might have been passed over with mild approval.

To get the balance true, let us admit that while
Shakespeare was an Elizabethan playwright he was—and
now is to us—predominantly something much more.
Therefore we had better not too unquestioningly thrust
him back within the confines his genius has escaped, nor

presume him to have felt the pettier circumstances of his theatre sacrosanct. Nor can we turn Elizabethans as we watch the plays; and every mental effort to do so will subtract from our enjoyment of them. This is the case against the circumstantial reproduction of Shakespeare's staging. But Mr Poel's achievement remains; he cleared for us from Shakespeare's stagecraft the scenic rubbish by which it had been so long encumbered and disguised. And we could now, if we would, make a promising fresh start. For the scholars, on their side, have lately—the scholarly among them—cut clear of the transcendental fog (scenic illusion of another sort) in which their nine-teenth-century peers loved to lose themselves, and they too are beginning again at the beginning. A text acquires virtue now by its claim to be a prompt book, and the most comprehensive work of our time upon the Elizabethan stage is an elaborate sorting-out of plays, companies and theatres. On Dr Pollard's treatment of the texts and on the foundations of fact laid by Sir Edmund Chambers a new scholarship is rising, aiming first to see Shakespeare in the theatre for which he wrote. It is a scholarship, therefore, by which the theatre of today can profit, to which, by its acting of Shakespeare, it could contribute, one would hope. Nor should the scholars disdain the help; for criticism cannot live upon criticism, it needs refreshment from the living art. Besides, what is all the criticism and scholarship finally for if not to keep Shakespeare alive? And he must always be most alive—even if roughly and rudely alive—in the theatre. Let the scholars force a way in there, if need be. Its fervid atmosphere will do them good; the benefit will be mutual.

These Prefaces are an attempt to profit by this new scholarship and to contribute to it some research into Shakespeare's stagecraft, by examining the plays, one after another, in the light of the interpretation he designed for them, so far as this can be deduced; to discover, if possible, the production he would have desired for them, all merely incidental circumstances apart. They might profit more written a generation hence, for the ground they build upon is still far from clear. And this introduction is by no means a conspectus of the subject; that can only come as a sequel. There has been, in this branch of Shakespearean study, too much generalization and far too little analysis of material.[2]

Shakespeare's Stagecraft

SHAKESPEARE'S own career was not a long one. The whole history of the theatre he wrote for does not cover a century. Between Marlowe and Massinger, from the first blaze to the glowing of the embers, it is but fifty years. Yet even while Shakespeare was at work, the stage to which he fitted his plays underwent constant and perhaps radical change. From Burbage's first theatre to the Globe, then to Blackfriars, not to mention excursions to Court and into the great halls—change of audiences and their behaviour, of their taste, development of the art of acting, change of the stage itself and its resources were all involved in the progress, and are all, we may be sure, reflected to some degree in the plays themselves. We guess at the conditions of each sort of stage and theatre, but there is often the teasing question to which of them had a play, as we have it now, been adapted. And of the 'private' theatre, most in vogue for the ten years preceding the printing of the First Folio so far we know least. The dating of texts and their ascription to the usages of a particular theatre may often be a searchlight upon their stagecraft. Here is much work for the new scholarship.

Conversely, the watchful working-out of the plays in action upon this stage or that would be of use to the scholars, who otherwise must reconstruct their theatre and gloss their texts as in a vacuum. The play was once fitted to the stage; it is by no means impossible to rebuild that stage now, with its doors, balconies, curtains and machines, by measuring the needs of the play. It is idle, for instance, to imagine scenes upon inner or upper stage without evidence that they will be audible or visible there; and editing is still vitiated by lack of this simple knowledge. Here, if nowhere else, this present research must fall short, for its method should rightly be experimental; more than one mind should be at work on it, moreover.

The text of a play is a score waiting performance, and the performance and its preparation are, almost from the beginning, a work of collaboration. A producer may direct the preparation, certainly. But if he only knows how to give orders, he has mistaken his vocation; he had better be a drill-sergeant. He might talk to his company when they all met together for the first time to study *Love's Labour's Lost, Julius Cæsar* or *King Lear*, on some such lines as these Prefaces pursue, giving a considered opinion of the play, drawing a picture of it in action, providing, in fact, a hypothesis which mutual study would prove—and might partly disprove. No sort of study of a play can better the preparation of its performance if this is rightly done. The matured art of the playwright lies in giving life to characters in action, and the secret of it in giving each character a due chance in the battle, the action of a play becoming literally the fighting of a battle of character. So the greater the playwright, the wider and deeper his sympathies, the more genuine this opposition will be and the less easily will a single mind grasp it, as it must be grasped, in the fullness of its emotion. The dialogue of a play runs—and often intricately—upon lines of reason, but it is charged besides with an emotion which speech releases, yet only releases fully when the speaker is—as an actor is—identified with the character. There is further the incidental action, implicit in the dialogue, which springs to life only when a scene is in being. A play, in fact, as we find it written, is a magic spell; and even the magician cannot always foresee the full effect of it.

Not every play, it must be owned, will respond to such intensive study. Many, ambitiously conceived, would collapse under the strain. Many are mere occasions for display of their actors' wit or eloquence, good looks or nice behaviour, and meant to be no more; and if they are skilfully contrived the parts fit together and the whole machine should go like clockwork. Nor, in fact, are even the greatest plays often so studied. There is hardly a theatre in the world where masterpiece and trumpery alike are not rushed through rehearsals to an arbitrarily effective performance, little more learned of them than the words, gaps in the understanding of them filled up with 'business'—effect without cause, the demand for this being the curse of the theatre as of other arts, as of other things than art. Not to such treatment will the greater plays of Shakespeare yield their secrets. But working upon a stage which reproduced the essential conditions of his, working as students, not as showmen merely, a company of actors might well find many of the riddles of the library answering themselves unasked. And these Prefaces could best be a record of such work, if such work were to be done.

We cannot, on the other hand, begin our research by postulating the principles of the Elizabethan stage. One is tempted to say it had none, was too much a child of nature to bother about such things. Principles were doubtless imposed upon it when it reached respectability, and heads would be bowed to the yoke. Shakespeare's among them? He had served a most practical apprenticeship to his trade. If he did not hold horses at the door, he sat behind the curtains, we may be sure, and held the prompt book on occasion. He acted, he cobbled other men's plays, he could write his own to order. Such a one may stay a journeyman if he is not a genius, but he will not become a doctrinaire. Shakespeare's work shows such principles as the growth of a tree shows. It is not haphazard merely because it is not formal; it is shaped by inner strength. The theatre, as he found it, allowed him and encouraged him to great freedom of development. Because the material resources of a stage are simple, it does not follow that the technique of its playwriting will stay so. Crude work may show up more crudely, when there are none of the fal-lals of illusion to disguise it that the modern theatre provides. But, if he has it in him, a dramatist can, so unfettered, develop the essentials of his art more boldly and more subtly too. The Elizabethan drama made an amazingly quick advance from crudity to an excellence which was often technically most elaborate. The advance and the not less amazing gulf which divides its best from its worst may be ascribed to the simplicity of the machinery it employed. That its decadence was precipitated by the influence of the Masque and the shifting of its centre of interest from the barer public stage to the candle-lit private theatre, where the machinery of the Masque became effective, it would be rash to assert; but the occurrences are suspiciously related. Man and machine (here at any rate is a postulate, if a platitude!) are false allies in the theatre, secretly at odds; and when man gets the worst of it, drama is impoverished; and the struggle, we may add, is perennial. No great drama depends upon pageantry. All great drama tends to concentrate upon character; and, even so, not upon picturing men as they show themselves to the world like figures on a stage—though that is how it must ostensibly show them—but on the hidden man. And the progress of Shakespeare's art from *Love's Labour's Lost* to *Hamlet*, and thereafter with a difference, lies in the simplifying of this paradox and the solving of the problem it presents; and the process involves the developing of a very subtle sort of stagecraft indeed.

For one result we have what we may call a very self-contained drama. Its chief values, as we know, have not changed with the fashions of the theatre. It relies much on the music of the spoken word, and a company of schoolchildren with pleasant voices, and an ear for rhythm, may vociferate through a play to some effect. It is as much to be enjoyed in the reading, if we hear it in imagination as we read, as drama meant to be acted can be. As with its simplicities then, so it should be, we presume, with its complexities. The subtly emotional use of verse and the interplay of motive and character, can these not be appreciated apart from the bare boards of their original setting? It does not follow. It neither follows that the advantages of the Elizabethan stage were wholly negative nor that, with our present knowledge, we can imagine the full effect of a play in action upon it. The imagining of a play in action is, under no circumstances, an easy thing.[3] What would one not give to go backward through the centuries to see the first performance of *Hamlet*, played as Shakespeare had it played![4] In default, if we could but make ourselves read it as if it were a manuscript fresh from its author's hands! There is much to be said for turning one's back on the editors, even, when possible, upon the First Folio with its demarcation of acts and scenes, in favour of the Quartos—Dr Pollard's 'good' Quartos—in their yet greater simplicity.

The Convention of Place

IT is, for instance, hard to discount the impression made merely by reading: *Scene i—Elsinore. A platform before the Castle*; and most of us have, to boot, early memories of painted battlements and tenth-century castles (of ageing Hamlets and their portly mothers for that matter) very difficult to dismiss. No great harm, one protests; it was a help, perhaps, to the unimaginative. But it is a first step to the certain misunderstanding of Shakespeare's stagecraft. The 'if, how and when' of the presenting of localities on the Elizabethan stage is, of course, a complex question. Shakespeare himself seems to have followed, consciously, no principles in the matter, nor was his practice very logical, nor at all consistent. It may vary with the play he is writing and the particular stage he is writing for; it will best be studied in relation to each play. We can, however, free ourselves from one general misconception which belongs to our own over-logical standpoint. When we learn with a shock of surprise—having begun in the schoolroom upon the Shakespeare of the editors, it comes as belated news to us—that neither battlements, throne rooms nor picturesque churchyards were to be seen at the Globe, and that *Elsinore. A platform before the Castle* is not Shakespeare at all, we yet imagine ourselves among the audience there busily conjuring these things up before the eye of faith. The Elizabethan audience was at no such pains. Nor was this their alternative to seeing the actors undisguisedly concerned with the doors, curtains and balconies which, by the play's requirements, should have been anything but what they were. As we, when a play has no hold on us, may fall to thinking about the scenery, so to a Globe audience, unmoved, the stage might be an obvious bare stage. But are we conscious of the scenery behind the actor when the play really moves us? If we are, there is something very wrong with the scenery, which should know its place as a background. The audience was not conscious of curtain and balcony when Burbage played Hamlet to them. They were conscious of Hamlet. That conventional background faded as does our painted illusion, and they certainly did not deliberately conjure up in its place mental pictures of Elsinore. The genus audience is passive, if expectant, imaginatively lazy till roused, never, one may be sure, at pains to make any effort that is generally unnecessary to enjoyment.

With Shakespeare the locality of a scene has dramatic importance, or it has none; and this is as true of his early plays as his late ones. Both in *Richard II* and *Antony and Cleopatra*, scene after scene passes with no exact indication of where we may be. With *Cleopatra* we are surely in Egypt, with Cæsar in Rome. Pompey appears, and the talk tells us that both Egypt and Rome are elsewhere; but positively where Pompey is at the moment we never learn.[5] Indoors or outdoors? The action of the scene or the clothing of the characters will tell us this if we need to know. But, suddenly transported to the Parthian war, our whereabouts is made amply plain. It is, however, made plain by allusion. The information peeps out through talk of kindred things; we are hardly aware we are being told, and, again, we learn no more than we need to learn. This, truly, is a striking development from the plump and plain

> Barkloughly Castle call they this at hand?

of Richard II, even from the more descriptive

> I am a stranger here in Gloucestershire:
> These high wild hills and rough, uneven ways
> Draw out our miles. . .

by which Shakespeare pictures and localizes the manoeuvres of Richard and Bolingbroke when he wants to.
But the purpose is the same, and the method essentially
the same.[6] Towards the end of the later play come scene
after scene of the marching and countermarching of
armies, of fighting, of truce, all the happenings of three
days' battle. Acts III and IV contain twenty-eight scenes
long and short; some of them are very short; three of
them have but four lines apiece. The editors conscien-
tiously ticket them *A plain near Actium, Another part of the
plain, Another part of the plain* and so on, and conclude that
Shakespeare is really going too far and too fast, is indeed
(I quote Sir Edmund Chambers) 'in some danger of
outrunning the apprehensions of his auditory.' Indeed he
might be if this cinematographic view of his intentions
were the right one! But it utterly falsifies them. Show an
audience such a succession of painted scenes—if you
could at the pace required—and they would give attention to nothing else whatever; the drama would pass
unnoticed. Had Shakespeare tried to define the whereabouts of every scene in any but the baldest phrases—the
protesting editors seem not to see that he makes no
attempt to; only *they* do!—he would have had to lengthen
and complicate them; had he written only a labelling
line or two he would still have distracted his audience
from the essential drama. Ignoring whereabouts, letting
it at most transpire when it naturally will, the characters
capture all attention. This is the true gain of the bare
stage; unless to some dramatic end no precious words
need be spent, in complying with the undramatic demands of space and time; incarnation of character can
be all in all. Given such a crisis as this the gain is yet
greater. We are carried through the phases of the three
days' battle; and what other stage convention would
allow us so varied a view of it, could so isolate the true

drama of it? For do we not pass through such a crisis in reality with just that indifference to time and place? These scenes, in their kind, show Shakespeare's stagecraft, not at its most reckless, but at its very best, and exemplify perfectly the freedom he enjoyed that the stage of visual illusion has inevitably lost. His drama is attached solely to its actors and their acting; that, perhaps, puts it in a phrase. They carry place and time with them as they move. The modern theatre still accepts the convention that measures time more or less by a play's convenience; a half-hour stands for an hour or more, and we never question the vagary. It was no more strange to an Elizabethan audience to see a street in Rome turned, in the use made of it, to the Senate House by the drawing of a curtain and the disclosure of Cæsar's state, to find Cleopatra's Monument now on the upper stage because Antony had to be drawn up to it, later on the lower because Cleopatra's death-scene could best be played there; it would seem that they were not too astonished even when Juliet, having taken leave of Romeo on the balcony of her bedroom and watched him descend to the lower stage, the scene continuing, came down, a few lines later, to the lower stage herself, bringing, so to speak, her bedroom with her—since this apparently is what she must have done.[7] For neither Senate House, Monument nor balcony had rights and reality of their own. They existed for the convenience of the actors, whose touch gave them life, a shadowy life at most; neglected, they existed no longer.[8]

Shakespeare's stagecraft concentrates, and inevitably, upon opportunity for the actor. We think now of the plays themselves; their first public knew them by their acting; and the development of the actor's art from the agilities and funniments of the clown, and from round-mouthed rhetoric to imaginative interpreting of character by such standards as Hamlet set up for his players, was a factor in the drama's triumph that we now too often ignore. Shakespeare himself, intent more and more upon plucking out the heart of the human mystery, stimulated his actors to a poignancy and intimacy of emotional expression—still can stimulate them to it—as no other playwright has quite learned to do.

The Speaking of the Verse

His verse was, of course, his chief means to this emotional expression; and when it comes to staging the plays, the speaking of verse must be the foundation of all study. The changes of three hundred years have of themselves put difficulties in our way here; though there are some besides—as one imagines—of Shakespeare's own making. Surely his syntax must now and then have puzzled even his contemporaries. Could they have made much more than we can of Leontes'

> Affection! thy intention stabs the centre;
> Thou dost make possible things not so held,
> Communicat'st with dreams;—How can this be?
> With what's unreal thou coactive art,
> And fellow'st nothing; then, 'tis very credent
> Thou may'st co-join with something; and thou dost;
> And that beyond commission; and I find it,
> And that to the infection of my brains,
> And hardening of my brows.

The confusion of thought and intricacy of language is dramatically justified. Shakespeare is picturing a genuinely jealous man (the sort of man that Othello was *not*) in the grip of a mental epilepsy. We parse the passage and dispute its sense; spoken, as it was meant to be, in a choking torrent of passion, probably a modicum of sense slipped through, and its first hearers did not find it a mere rigmarole. But we are apt to miss even that much. Other passages, of early and late writing, may always have had as much sound as sense to them; but now, to the casual hearer, they will convey more sound than sense by far. Nor do puns mean to us what they meant to the Elizabethans, delighting in their language for its own sake. Juliet's tragic fantasia upon 'Aye' and 'I' sounds all but ridiculous, and one sympathizes with an actress hesitating to venture on it. How far, apart from the shifting of accents and the recolouring of vowels, has not the whole habit of English speech changed in these three hundred years? In the theatre it was slowing down, one fancies, throughout the eighteenth century; and in the nineteenth, as far as Shakespeare was concerned, it grew slower and slower, till on occasions one thought—even hoped—that shortly the actor would stop altogether. There may have been more than one cause; imitation of the French Augustans, the effort to make antiquated phrases understood, the increasing size of the theatres themselves would all contribute to it. The result, in any case, is disastrous. Elizabethan drama was built upon vigour and beauty of speech. The groundlings may often have deserved Shakespeare's strictures, but they would stand in discomfort for an hour or so to be stirred by the sound of verse. Some of the actors no doubt were robustious periwig-pated fellows, but, equally, it was no empty ideal of acting he put into Hamlet's mouth—and Burbage's. We may suppose that at its best the mere speaking of the plays was a very brilliant thing, compared to *bel canto*, or to a pianist's virtuosity. The emotional appeal of our modern music was in it, and it could be tested by ears trained to the rich and delicate fretwork of the music of that day. Most Hamlets—not being playwrights—make a mild joke of telling us they'd as lief the town-crier spoke their lines, but we may hear in it the echo of some of Shakespeare's sorest trials.

The speaking of his verse must be studied, of course, in relation to the verse's own development. The actor must not attack its supple complexities in *Antony and Cleopatra* and *Cymbeline*, the mysterious dynamics of *Macbeth*, the nobilities of *Othello*, its final pastoral simplicities in *A Winter's Tale* and *The Tempest* without preliminary training in the lyricism, the swift brilliance and the masculine clarity of the earlier plays. A modern actor, alas, thinks it simple enough to make his way, splay-footed, through

The cloud-capped towers, the gorgeous palaces . . .

though Berowne's

I, forsooth, in love . . .

or one of Oberon's apostrophes will defeat him utterly. And, without an ear trained to the delicacy of the earlier work, his hearers, for their part, will never know how shamefully he is betraying the superb ease of the later. If we are to make Shakespeare our own again we must all be put to a little trouble about it. We must recapture as far as may be his lost meanings; and the sense of a phrase we *can* recapture, though instinctive emotional response to it may be a loss forever. The tunes that he writes to, the whole great art of his music-making, we can master. Actors can train their ears and tongues and can train our ears to it. We talk of lost arts. No art is ever lost while the means to it survive. Our faculties rust by disuse and by misuse are coarsened, but they quickly recover delight in a beautiful thing. Here, at any rate, is the touchstone by which all interpreting of Shakespeare the playwright must first—and last—be tried.

The Boy-Actress

MORE than one of the conditions of his theatre made this medium of accomplished speech of such worth to him. Boys played the women parts; and what could a boy bring to Juliet, Rosalind or Cleopatra beyond grace of manner and charm of speech? We have been used to women on the stage for two hundred and fifty years or more, and a boy Juliet—if the name on the programme revealed one, for nothing else might—would seem an odd fish to us; no one would risk a squeaking Cleopatra; though, as for Rosalind, through three-parts of the play a boy would have the best of it. But the parts were written for boys; not, therefore, without consideration of how boys could act them most convincingly. Hence, of course, the popularity of the heroine so disguised. The disguise was perfect; the make-believe one degree more complex, certainly, than it needs to be with us; but once you start make-believe it matters little how far you go with it; there is, indeed, some enjoyment in the make-believe itself. But, further, it is Shakespeare's constant care to demand nothing of a boy-actress that might turn to unseemliness or ridicule. He had not much taste for what is called 'domestic drama,' nor does he dose us very heavily with Doll Tearsheet, Mistress Overdone and their like. Constance mourns Arthur's loss, Lady Macduff has her little son, but no mother croons over the child in her arms. Paulina brings Hermione's baby to Leontes, it is true; but see with what tact, from this point of view, the episode is managed. And love-scenes are most carefully contrived. Romeo and Juliet are seldom alone together; never for long, but in the balcony-scene; and in this, the most famous of love-scenes, they are kept from all contact with each other. Consider *Antony and*

Cleopatra. Here is a tragedy of sex without one single scene of sexual appeal. That aspect of Cleopatra is reflected for us in talk about her; mainly by Enobarbus, who is not mealymouthed; but his famed description of her voluptuousness is given us when she has been out of our sight for several scenes. The play opens with her parting from Antony, and in their two short encounters we see her swaying him by wit, malice and with the moods of her mind. Not till the story takes its tragic plunge and sex is drowned in deeper passion are they ever intimately together; till he is brought to her dying there has been occasion for but one embrace. Contrast this with a possible Cleopatra planned to the advantage of the actress of today.

Shakespeare, artist that he was, turned this limitation to account, made loss into a gain.[9] Feminine charm—of which the modern stage makes such capital—was a medium denied him. So his men and women encounter upon a plane where their relation is made rarer and intenser by poetry, or enfranchised in a humour which surpasses more primitive love-making. And thus, perhaps, he was helped to discover that the true stuff of tragedy and of the liveliest comedy lies beyond sensual bounds. His studies of women seem often to be begun from some spiritual paces beyond the point at which a modern dramatist leaves off. Curious that not a little of the praise lavished upon the beauty and truth of them— mainly by women—may be due to their having been written to be played by boys!

Much could be said for the restoring of the celibate stage; but the argument, one fears, would be academic. Here, though, is practical counsel. Let the usurping actress remember that her sex is a liability, not an asset. The dramatist of today may refuse to exploit its allure-ments, but may legitimately allow for the sympathetic effect of it; though the less he does so, perhaps, the better for his play and the more gratitude the better sort of actress will show him. But Shakespeare makes no such demands, has left no blank spaces for her to fill with her charm. He asks instead for self-forgetful clarity of perception, and for a sensitive, spirited, athletic beauty of speech and conduct, which will leave prettiness and its lures at a loss, and the crudities of more Circean appeal looking very crude indeed.

The Soliloquy

THIS convention of the boy-actress may be said to give a certain remoteness to a play's acting. The soliloquy brings a compensating intimacy, and its use was an important part of Shakespeare's stagecraft. Its recognized usefulness was for the disclosing of the plot, but he soon improved upon this. Soliloquy becomes the means by which he brings us not only to a knowledge of the more secret thoughts of his characters, but into the closest emotional touch with them too. Here the platform stage helped him, as the stage of scenic illusion now defeats his purpose. But it is not altogether a question of 'realism' and the supposed obligation this lays upon a real man in a real-looking room to do nothing he would not do if the whole affair were real.

There is no escape from convention in the theatre, and all conventions can be made acceptable, though they cannot all be used indiscriminately, for they are founded in the physical conditions of the stage of their origin and are often interdependent one with another. Together they form a code, and they are as a treaty made with the audience. No article of it is to be abrogated unless we can be persuaded to consent, and upon its basis we surrender our imaginations to the playwright.

With the soliloquy upon the platform stage it is a case—as so often where convention is concerned—of extremes meeting. There is no illusion, so there is every illusion. Nothing very strange about this man, not even the dress he wears, leaning forward a little we could touch him; we are as intimate and familiar with him as it is possible to be. We agree to call him 'Hamlet', to suppose that he is where he says he is, we admit that he thinks aloud and in blank verse too. It is possible that the more we are asked to imagine the easier we find it to do. It is certain that, once our imagination is working, visual illusion will count for little in the stimulating of emotion beside this intimacy that allows the magnetism of personality full play.

There is no more important task for the producer of Shakespeare than to restore to the soliloquy its rightful place in a play's economy, and in particular to regain for it full emotional effect. We now accept the convention frigidly, the actor manoeuvres with it timidly. Banished behind footlights into that other world of illusion, the solitary self-communing figure rouses our curiosity at best. Yet further adapted to the self-contained methods of modern acting, the soliloquy has quite inevitably become a slack link in the play's action, when it should be a recurring reinforcement to its strength. Shakespeare never pinned so many dramatic fortunes to a merely utilitarian device. Time and again he may be feeling his way through a scene for a grip on his audience, and it is the soliloquy ending it that will give him—and his actor—the stranglehold. When he wishes to quicken the pulse of the action, to screw up its tension in a second or so, the soliloquy serves him well. For a parallel to its full effectiveness on Shakespeare's stage we should really look to the modern music-hall comedian getting on terms with his audience. We may measure the response to Burbage's

O, that this too too solid flesh would melt . . .

by recalling—those of us that happily can—Dan Leno as a washerwoman, confiding domestic troubles to a theatre full of friends, and taken unhindered to their hearts. The problem is not really a difficult one. If we solve the physical side of it by restoring, in essentials, the relation between actor and audience that the intimacy of the platform stage provided, the rest should soon solve itself.

Costume

THE problem of costume, when it arises, is a subtler one; nor probably is it capable of any logical solution. Half the plays can be quite appropriately dressed in the costume of Shakespeare's own time. It is a false logic which suggests that to match their first staging we should dress them in the costume of ours. For with costume goes custom and manners—or the lack of them. It may be both a purge and a tonic to the sluggish-fancied spectator to be shown a Prince of Denmark in coat and trousers and a Grave-digger in a bowler hat, for reminder that here is a play, not a collection of ritualized quotations. But physic is for the sick; also, there may be less drastic cures. When archaeology took hold upon the nineteenth-century mind it became a matter of moment to lodge Hamlet in historic surroundings; and withers were wrung by the anachronisms of ducats and a murder of Gonzago, French rapiers and the rest. A needlessly teasing difficulty; why reproduce it in terms of a young man in a dinner jacket searching for a sword—a thing not likely to be lying about in his modern mother's sitting room—with which to kill Polonius, who certainly has window curtains to hide behind instead of arras? This gain of intimacy—with a Hamlet we might find sitting opposite at a dinner party—may well be a gain in sympathy. It was originally a great gain, a gift to Shakespeare's audience. But we pay too high a price for it.

What was the actual Elizabethan practice in this matter of costuming is not comprehensively known. We can only say safely that, as with other matters, it was neither constant, consistent, nor, from our present point of view, rational. It was based upon the use of the clothes of the time; but these might be freely and fantastically adapted to suit a particular play or advantage some character in it. Dramatic effect was probably the first consideration and the last. There were such fancy dresses as Oberon or Puck or Caliban might wear; there was always the symbolizing of royalty, and a king would wear a crown whenever he could; there was the utility of knowing Romans from Britons by sight in *Cymbeline*, the martial Roman from the effete Egyptian in *Antony and Cleopatra*, and a Scottish lord when you saw him in *Macbeth*, if we may judge by Malcolm's comment upon Rosse's appearance:

> My countryman; and yet I know him not.

Our difficulty, of course, arises mainly over the historical plays. Not over the English Histories, even so; we can dress Richard III or Henry V by the light of our own superior knowledge of what they wore, and never find it clash violently with anything Shakespeare has put on their backs or in their mouths. But when we come to Julius Cæsar plucking open his doublet, to the conspirators against him with their hats about their ears, and to Cleopatra's

> Cut my lace, Charmian.

not to mention British Imogen in her doublet and hose, we must stop and consider.

The common practice is, in these instances, to ignore the details of Shakespeare's text altogether; to dress Cæsar in his toga, Cleopatra in her habit as she lived, with never a stay-lace about her (though, truly, the costumier, let alone, will tend to get his fashion a few thousand years wrong and turn her out more like the wife of Tutankhamen); and as to Imogen and her surroundings, we do our best to compromise with skins and woad. This may be a lesser evil than presenting a Cæsar recalling Sir Walter Raleigh and a Cleopatra who would make us think of Mary Queen of Scots, but it is no solution of the problem. For the actors have to speak these lines, and if action and appearance contradict them, credibility is destroyed. And the constant credibility of the actor must be a producer's first care. Nor is this all, nor is it, perhaps, the most important thing to consider. The plays are full of reference, direct and indirect, to Elizabethan custom. They are, further, impregnated with what we call 'Renaissance feeling', some more, some less, but all to a degree. Now of this last we have a sense which is likelier to be a better help to their appreciation than any newfangled knowledge of the correct cut of Cleopatra's clothes will be! We know Iago for a Machiavellian figure (so called), and miss none of Shakespeare's intention. But if ever two men breathed the air of a sixteenth-century court, Hamlet and Claudius of Denmark do, and to relate them in habit and behaviour to the twilight figures of Saxo Grammaticus is as much a misinterpretation as any mauling of the text can be. They exist essentially doubtless—as do all the major characters of the plays—in their perennial humanity. But never let us forget the means by which this deeper truth of them is made vivid and actual. There have been better intellects than Shakespeare's, and poetry as good as his. He holds his supreme place by

his dramatist's necessary power of bringing thought and
vague emotion to the terms of action and convincing
speech; further, and far more than is often allowed, by
his peculiar gift of bringing into contribution the com-
mon-place traffic of life. However wide the spoken word
may range, there must be the actor, anchored to
the stage. However high, then, with Shakespeare, the
thought or emotion may soar, we shall always find the
transcendental set in the familiar. He keeps this balance
constantly adjusted; and, at his play's greatest moments,
when he must make most sure of our response, he will
employ the simplest means. The higher arguments of the
plays are thus kept always within range, and their rooted
humanity blossoms in a fertile upspringing of expressive
little things. Neglect or misinterpret these, the inner
wealth of Shakespeare will remain, no doubt, and we
may mine for it, but we shall have levelled his landscape
bare.

Shakespeare's own attitude in this matter of costume
and customs was as inconsistent as his practice was
casual. He knew what *his* Cæsar or Cleopatra would be
wearing and would casually drop in a reference to it.
Yet the great Romans themselves were aliens to him.
The great idea of Rome fired his imagination. Brutus,
Cassius and Antony do not turn typical Elizabethan
gentlemen; and to the end of that play he is striving to
translate Plutarch. Whenever, on the other hand, even
for a moment he has made a character all his own, he
cannot but clothe it in lively familiar detail. Cleopatra's
are the coquetries of a great lady of his own time, in
their phrasing, in the savour. When the heights of the
tragedy have to be scaled, manners will not so much
matter. But if we make her, at the play's beginning, a
pseudo-classic, languishing Oriental, we must do it in
spite of Shakespeare, not by his help. What then is the

solution of this problem, if the sight of the serpent of old Nile in a farthingale will too dreadfully offend us? We can compromise. Look at Tintoretto's and Paolo Veronese's paintings of 'classic' subjects. We accept them readily enough.

Sometimes, within the boundaries of a play, the centuries seem all at odds. *Cymbeline* need not trouble us, its Roman Britain is pure 'once upon a time'. But in *King Lear*, for instance, Shakespeare is at unwonted pains to throw us back into some heathen past. Yet Edmund is another Iago, Edgar might have been at Wittenberg with Hamlet, and Oswald steps straight from the seventeenth-century London streets. Here, though, the dominant barbarism is the important thing; the setting for Goneril and Regan, Lear's tyranny and madness, and Gloucester's blinding. To a seventeenth-century audience Oswald was so identifiable a figure that it would not matter greatly how he dressed; the modern designer of costume must show him up as best he may. Each play, in fine, if it presents a problem at all, presents its own.

The Integrity of the Text

THE text, one says at first blush, can present no problem at all. The plays should be acted as Shakespeare wrote them—how dispute it? They should be; and it is as well, before we discuss hard cases, to have the principle freely admitted. Lip service enough is done it nowadays, and Colley Cibber's *Richard III*, Tate's *Lear* and Garrick's improvements are at the back of our bookshelves, but we still find Messrs John Doe and Richard Roe slicing out lines by the dozen and even a scene or so, or chopping and changing them to suit their scenery. This will not do. Shakespeare was not a perfect playwright; there can be no such thing. Nor did he aim at a mechanical perfection, but a vitality, and this he achieved. At best then, we cut and carve the body of a play to its peril. It may be robustly, but it may be very delicately organized. And we still know little enough of the laws of its existence, and some of us, perhaps, are not such very skilful surgeons; nor is any surgeon to be recommended who operates for his own convenience.

This good rule laid down, what are the exceptions that go to prove it? There is the pornographic difficulty. This is not such a stumbling block to us as it was to Bowdler, to some bright young eyes nowadays it is quite imperceptible, in fact. Yet, saving their presence, it exists; for it exists aesthetically. Shakespeare's characters often make obscene jokes. The manners of his time permitted it. The public manners of ours still do not. Now the dramatic value of a joke is to be measured by its effect upon an audience, and each is meant to make its own sort of effect. If then, instead of giving them a passing moment's amusement, it makes a thousand people uncomfortable and for the next five minutes very self-conscious, it fails of its true effect. This argument must not be stretched to cover the silliness of turning 'God' into 'Heaven' and of making Othello call Desdemona a 'wanton' (the practice, as I recollect, of the eighteen-nineties), nor to such deodorizing of *Measure for Measure* that it becomes hard to discover what all the fuss is about. If an audience cannot think of Angelo and the Duke, Pompey and Lucio, Isabella and Mistress Overdone, and themselves to boot, as fellow-creatures all, the play is not for them. Othello must call Desdemona a 'whore', and let those that do not like it leave the theatre; what have such queasy minds to do with the pity and terror of her murder and his death? Again, to make Beatrice so mealymouthed that she may not tell us how the devil is to meet her at the gates of hell, 'like an old cuckold with horns on his head', is to dress her in a crinoline, not a farthingale. But suppression of a few of the more scabrous jokes will not leave a play much the poorer; nor, one may add, will the average playgoer be much the wiser or merrier for hearing them, since they are often quite hard to understand.

Topical passages are a similar difficulty. With their savour, if not their very meaning lost, they show like dead wood in the living tree of the dialogue and are better, one would suppose, cut away. But no hard and fast rule will apply. Macbeth's porter's farmer and equivocator will never win spontaneous laughter again. But we cannot away with them, or nothing is left of the porter. Still the baffled low comedian must not, as his wont is, obscure the lines with bibulous antics. There will be that little dead spot in the play, and nothing can be done about it. Rosencrantz' reference to the 'eyrie of children' is meaningless except to the student. Is the play the poorer for the loss of it? But the logic that will take this out had better not rob us of

> Dead shepherd, now I find thy saw of might;
> Who ever loved that loved not at first sight?

And there is the strange case of

The lady of the Strachy married the yeoman of the wardrobe.

Nobody knows what it means, but everybody finds it funny when it is spoken in its place. And this has its parallels.

In general, however, better play the plays as we find them. The blue pencil is a dangerous weapon; and its use grows on a man, for it solves too many little difficulties far too easily.

Lastly, for a golden rule, whether staging or costuming or cutting is in question, and a comprehensive creed, a producer might well pin this on his wall: Gain Shakespeare's effects by Shakespeare's means when you can; for, plainly, this will be the better way. But gain Shakespeare's effects; and it is your business to discern them.

1927

Notes

1 But it should not be forgotten that Sir Herbert Tree, happy in the orthodoxy of public favour, welcomed the heretic Mr Poel more than once to a share in his Shakespeare Festivals.

2 I do not deal in general therefore with certain vexed questions, such as act-division, which still need to be looked at, I think, in the light of the particular play.

3 I remember a most intelligent reader of a modern play missing the whole point of a scene through which the chief character was to sit conspicuously and eloquently silent. He counted only with the written dialogue. I remember, when I thought I knew *King Lear* well enough, being amazed at the effect, all dialogue apart, of the mere meeting, when I saw it, of blind Gloucester and mad Lear.

4 Though, in a sense, there was no first performance of *Hamlet*. And doubtless many of the audience for Shakespeare's new version of the old play only thought he had spoiled a good story of murder and revenge by adding too much talk to it.

5 Unless it may be said that we learn in the scene after whereabouts he *was*.

6 And in *Coriolanus*, which probably postdates *Antony and Cleopatra*, with Marcius' 'A goodly city is this Antium,' we are back to the barely informative. It serves Shakespeare's purpose; he asks no more.

7 I fancy, though, that the later Shakespeare would have thought this a clumsy device.

8 How far this is true of other dramatists than Shakespeare I do not pretend to say; nor how far, with him, the influence of the private theatre, making undoubtedly towards the scenic stage

and (much later) for illusion, did not modify his practice, when he had that stage to consider. A question, again, for the bibliographers and historians.

9 There is no evidence, of course, that he felt it a loss, no such reference to the insufficiency of the boy-actress as there is to the overself-sufficiency of the clown. Women did appear in the Masques, if only to dance, so the gulf to be bridged was not a broad one. But the Elizabethan was as shocked by the notion of women appearing upon the public stage as the Chinese playgoer is today.

Romeo and Juliet

ROMEO AND JULIET is lyric tragedy, and this must be the key to its interpreting. It seems to have been Shakespeare's first unquestionable success, proof positive of his unique quality. If marred by one or two clumsy turns, its stagecraft is simple and sufficient; and the command of dramatic effect is masterly already. It is immature work still, but it is not crude. The writing shows us a Shakespeare skilled in devices that he is soon to reject or adapt to new purpose. This, which to the critic is one of the most interesting things about the play, is a stumbling block to its acting. But the passion and poignant beauty of it all, when we surrender ourselves to them, make such reservations of small enough account.

Whether we have the play as Shakespeare first wrote it may be doubted; we probably have it in the second Quarto as it last left his hands. But signs, as they may seem to be, of rewriting and retouching at one time or another, must always, in this or any of his plays, be warily viewed. They may, of course, be so obvious as to ask no proof; but when they depend on nice calculation one must remember that the critical foot-rule is poor measure for genius—and the very poorest for genius in its springtime.

The Mercutio of the Queen Mab speech is not, it can be argued, the Mercutio of

> No, 'tis not so deep as a well, nor so wide as a church-door; but 'tis enough, 'twill serve. . . .

Did the Juliet, one asks, of

> Hath Romeo slain himself? Say thou but 'I',
> And that bare vowel 'I' shall poison more
> Than the death-darting eye of cockatrice:
> I am not I, if there be such an 'I'. . . .

and the rest of the fantasia, turn within a sitting or so into the Juliet of

> Ancient damnation! O most wicked fiend!
> Is it more sin to wish me thus forsworn,
> Or to dispraise my lord with that same tongue
> Which she hath praised him with above compare
> So many thousand times?

and the Romeo of

> more courtship lives
> In carrion flies than Romeo: they may seize
> On the white wonder of dear Juliet's hand. . . .
> This may flies do, when I from this must fly. . . .

into the stark figure of the scene in Mantua, meeting the news of her death with

> Is it even so? Then I defy you, stars!

—into the Romeo who pays the apothecary with

> There is thy gold; worse poison to men's souls,
> Doing more murder in this loathsome world
> Than these poor compounds that thou mayst not sell:
> I sell thee poison, thou hast sold me none.

By all the rules, no doubt, there should be two Shakespeares at work here. But in such a ferment as we now find him (himself, in some sort, a young Romeo on the turn from a Rosaline of phrase-making to a deeper-welling love) he may well have been capable of working on Tuesday in one fashion, on Wednesday in another, capable of couplet, sonnet, word-juggling, straight sober verse, or hard-bitten prose, often as the popular story he was turning to account and the need of the actors for the thing they and he were so apt at seemed to demand, at times out of the new strength breeding in him. Our present concern, however, is with the play as we have it, and its interpreting in the theatre.

The Conduct of the Action

THE dominating merit of this is that Shakespeare takes Brooke's tale, and at once doubles its dramatic value by turning its months to days.

> These violent delights have violent ends. . . .

and a sense of swiftness belongs to them, too. A Hamlet may wait and wait for his revenge; but it accords with this love and its tragedy that four days should see its birth, consummation and end. Incidentally we can here see the 'Double Time'—which has so exercised the ingenuity of commentators, who will credit him with their own—slipping naturally and easily into existence.[1] He makes dramatic use of time when he needs to.

CAPULET. But soft, what day is this?
PARIS.   Monday, my lord.
CAPULET. Monday! Ha! ha! Well, Wednesday is too soon;
    O' Thursday let it be:—o' Thursday, tell her,
    She shall be married to this noble earl. . . .

This sense of the marriage looming but three days ahead is dramatically important; later to intensify it, he even lessens the interval by a day. But (his mind reverting now and then to Brooke's story as he read it, possibly before he saw that he must weave it closer) he will carelessly drop in phrases that are quite contradictory when we examine them. But what audience will examine them as they flash by?

> I anger her sometimes [says the Nurse to Romeo], and tell her that Paris is the properer man. . . .

(when neither Paris nor Romeo has been in the field for four and twenty hours).

> Is it more sin to wish me thus forsworn,
> Or to dispraise my lord with that same tongue
> Which she hath praised him with above compare
> So many thousand times?

(when, all allowance made for Juliet's exaggeration, the Nurse has not had twice twenty-four hours in which to praise or dispraise). But notice that this suggestion of the casual slackness of normal life conveniently loosens the tension of the tragedy a little. There is, indeed, less of carelessness than a sort of instinctive artistry about it; and the method is a natural by-product of the freedom of Shakespeare's theatre.

But he marshals his main action to very definite purpose. He begins it, not with the star-crossed lovers (though a prologue warns us of them), but with a clash of the two houses; and there is far more significance in this than lies in the fighting. The servants, not the masters, start the quarrel. If Tybalt is a firebrand, Benvolio is a peacemaker; and though Montague and Capulet themselves are drawn in, they have the grace to be a little ashamed after. The hate is cankered; it is an ancient quarrel set new abroach; and even the tetchy Capulet owns that it should not be so hard for men of their age to keep the peace. If it were not for the servants, then, who fight because they always have fought, and the Tybalts, who will quarrel about nothing

sooner than not quarrel at all, it is a feud ripe for
settling; everyone is weary of it; and no one more weary,
more impatient with it than Romeo;

> O me! What fray was here?
> Yet tell me not—for I have heard it all. . . .

We are not launching, then, into a tragedy of fated
disaster, but—for a more poignant if less highly heroic
theme—of opportunity muddled away and marred by
ill-luck. As a man of affairs, poor Friar Laurence proved
deplorable; but he had imagination. Nothing was likelier
than that the Montagues and Capulets, waking one morning to find Romeo and Juliet married, would have been
only too thankful for the excuse to stop killing each other.

> And the continuance of their parents' rage,
> Which, but their children's end, nought could remove . . .

says the Prologue. Nought in such a world as this,
surmises the young Shakespeare; in a world where

> I thought all for the best.

avails a hero little; for on the heels of it comes

> O, I am fortune's fool!

Having stated his theme, he develops it, as his habit
already is (and was to remain; the method so obviously
suits the continuities of the Elizabethan stage), by episodes of immediate contrast in character and treatment.
Thus, after the bracing rattle of the fight and the clarion
of the Prince's judgment, we have our first sight of
Romeo, fantastic, rueful, self-absorbed. His coming is
preluded by a long passage of word-music; and, that its
relevance may be plain, the verse slips into the tune of
it at the first mention of his name. Benvolio's brisk story
of the quarrel, dashed with irony, is finishing—

> While we were interchanging thrusts and blows,
> Came more and more, and fought on part and part,
> Till the Prince came, who parted either part.

—when Lady Montague interposes with

> O, where is Romeo? Saw you him to-day?
> Right glad am I he was not at this fray.

and promptly, like a change from wood-wind, brass and tympani to an andante on the strings, comes Benvolio's

> Madam, an hour before the worshipped sun
> Peered forth the golden window of the east . . .

Montague echoes him; and to the wooing smoothness of

> But he, his own affections' counsellor,
> Is to himself—I will not say how true—
> But to himself so secret and so close,
> So far from sounding and discovery,
> As is the bud bit with an envious worm,
> Ere he can spread his sweet leaves to the air,
> Or dedicate his beauty to the sun.
> Could we but learn from whence his sorrows grow,
> We would as willingly give cure as know.

Romeo appears; moody, oblivious of them all three. It is a piece of technique that belongs both to Shakespeare's stage in its simplicity and to the play's own lyrical cast.

Then (for contrasts of character and subject), close upon Romeo's mordant thought-play and word-play with Benvolio come Capulet and Paris, the sugary old tyrant and the man of wax, matchmaking—and such a good match for Juliet as it is to be! Close upon this comes Benvolio's wager that he'll show Romeo at the feast beauties to put Rosaline in the shade; and upon that, our first sight of Juliet, when she is bid take a liking to Paris at the feast if she can.

The scene of the procession of the Maskers to Capulet's house (with Romeo a spoil-sport as befits his mood) is unduly lengthened by the bravura of the Queen Mab speech, which is as much and as little to be dramatically justified as a song in an opera is.[2] But Shakespeare makes it serve to quicken the temper of the action to a pitch against which—as against the dance, too, and Tybalt's rage—Romeo's first encounter with Juliet will show with a quiet beauty all its own. Did he wonder for a moment how to make this stand out from everything else in the play? They share the speaking of a sonnet between them, and it is a charming device.

One must picture them there. The dance is over, the guests and the Maskers are in a little chattering, receding crowd, and the two find themselves alone.[3] Juliet would be for joining the others; but Romeo, his mask doffed, moves towards her, as a pilgrim towards a shrine.

> If I profane with my unworthiest hand . . .

It is hard to see what better first encounter could have been devised. To have lit mutual passion in them at once would have been commonplace; the cheapest of love tragedies might begin like that. But there is something sacramental in this ceremony, something shy and grave and sweet; it is a marriage made already. And she is such a child; touched to earnestness by his trembling earnestness, but breaking into fun at last (her defence when the granted kiss lights passion in him) as the last quatrain's metre breaks for its ending into

> You kiss by the book.

The tragedy to come will be deepened when we remember the innocence of its beginning. The encounter's

ending has significance too. They are not left to live in
a fool's paradise for long. Romeo hears who she is and
faces his fate. An hour ago he was affecting melancholy
while Mercutio and his fellows laughed round him. Now,
with the sport at its best, he braces to desperate reality.
Then, as the guests and Maskers depart and the laughter
dies, Juliet grows fearful. She hears her fate and must
face it, too.

> My only love sprung from my only hate!
> Too early seen unknown, and known too late!
> Prodigious birth of love it is to me
> That I must love a loathed enemy.

The child is no more a child.

A chorus follows. This may have some further function
than to fill up time while furniture is shifted or stage
fittings are adjusted; it is of no dramatic use.[4] Then
Romeo appears alone.

And now, with his finest stroke yet, all prepared and
pending (the love duet that is to be spoken from balcony
to garden), Shakespeare pauses to do still better by it;
and at the same time fits Mercutio to his true place in
the character scheme.[5] To appreciate the device we must
first forget the obliging editors with their *Scene i, A lane
by the wall of Capulet's orchard. Enter Romeo. . . . He climbs the
wall and leaps down within it. . . . Scene ii, Capulet's orchard.
Enter Romeo*—for all this has simply obliterated the effect.[6]
The *Enter Romeo alone* of the Quartos and Folio is the
only authentic stage direction concerning him. What
happens when Mercutio and Benvolio arrive in pursuit?
He hides somewhere about the stage. He has, they say,
'leapt this orchard wall'; but no wall is there, and—more
importantly—there is no break in the continuity of the
scene, now or later; it should be proof enough that to
make one we must cut a rhymed couplet in two. The

confusion of whereabouts, such as it is, that is involved, would not trouble the Elizabethans in the least; would certainly not trouble an audience that later on was to see Juliet play half a scene on the upper stage and half on the lower, with no particular change of place implied. The effect, so carefully contrived, lies in Romeo's being well within hearing of all the bawdry now to follow, which has no other dramatic point; and that the chaff is about the chaste Rosaline makes it doubly effective.

Dominating the stage with his lusty presence, vomiting his jolly indecencies, we see the sensual man, Mercutio; while in the background lurks Romeo, a-quiver at them, youth marked for tragedy.[7] His heart's agonizing after Rosaline had been real enough. He has forgotten that! But what awaits him now, with another heart, passionate as his own, to encounter? This is the eloquence of the picture, which is summed up in Romeo's rhyming end to the whole dithyramb as he steals out, looking after the two of them:

> He jests at scars that never felt a wound.

The discord thus struck is perfect preparation for the harmony to come; and Mercutio's ribaldry has hardly died from our ears before Juliet is at her window.

Throughout the famous scene Shakespeare varies and strengthens its harmony and sustains its drama by one small device after another. We must return to more careful study of it. At its finish, the brisk couplet,

> Hence will I to my ghostly father's cell,
> His help to crave, and my dear hap to tell.

brings us to earth again; and the action speeds on, to find a new helmsman in Friar Laurence. His importance to the play is made manifest by the length of his first soliloquy, and Shakespeare is looking forward already, we find, to the potion for Juliet. All goes smoothly and happily; the Friar is sententious, the lovers are ecstatic, Mercutio, Benvolio and the Nurse make a merry work-a-day chorus. Only that one note of warning is struck, lightly, casually:

> Tybalt, the kinsman of old Capulet,
> Hath sent a letter to his father's house.

The marriage-scene brings this 'movement' to its close.

FRIAR.   So smile the heavens upon this holy act,
   That after-hours with sorrow chide us not!
ROMEO. Amen, amen! But come what sorrow can,
   It cannot countervail the exchange of joy
   That one short minute gives me in her sight.
   Do thou but close our hands with holy words,
   Then love-devouring death do what he dare,
   It is enough I may but call her mine.
FRIAR.   These violent delights have violent ends,
   And in their triumph die. . . .

Youth triumphant and defiant, age sadly wise; a scene of quiet consummation, stillness before the storm. We are just halfway through the play.

> Come, come with me, and we will make short work;
> For, by your leaves, you shall not stay alone
> Till holy church incorporate two in one.

But upon this, in immediate, most significant contrast, there stride along Mercutio and Benvolio, swords on hip, armed servants following them, Mercutio with mischief enough a-bubble in him for the prudent Benvolio to be begging:

> I pray thee, good Mercutio, let's retire;
> The day is hot, the Capulets abroad,

> And if we meet we shall not scape a brawl,
> For now, these hot days, is the mad blood stirring.

—and (with one turn of the dramatist's wrist) tragedy is in train.[8]

The scene that follows is the most strikingly effective thing in the play. It comes quickly to its crisis when Romeo enters to encounter Tybalt face to face. For this moment the whole action has been preparing. Consider the constituents of the situation. Tybalt has seen Romeo eyeing his cousin Juliet from behind a mask and its privilege, and to no good purpose, be sure. But in Benvolio's and Mercutio's eyes he is still the lackadaisical adorer of Rosaline, a scoffer at the famous family quarrel suddenly put to the proof of manhood by a Capulet's insult. We know—we only—that he has even now come from his marriage to Juliet, from the marriage which is to turn these

> households' rancour to pure love.

The moment is made eloquent by a silence. For what is Romeo's answer to be to an insult so complete in its sarcastic courtesy?

> Romeo, the love I bear thee can afford
> No better term than this: Thou art a villain.

Benvolio and Mercutio, Tybalt himself, have no doubt of it; but to us the silence that follows—its lengthening by one pulse-beat mere amazement to them—is all suspense. We know what is in the balance. The moment is, for Romeo, so packed with emotions that the actor may interpret it in half a dozen ways, each legitimate (and by such an endowment we may value a dramatic situation). Does he come from his 'one short minute' with Juliet so rapt in happiness that the sting of the insult cannot pierce him, that he finds himself contemplating this Tybalt and his inconsequent folly unmoved? Does he flash into passion and check it, and count the cost to his pride and the scorn of his friends, and count them as nothing, all in an instant? Whatever the effect on him, we, as we watch, can interpret it, no one else guessing. And when he does answer:

> Tybalt, the reason that I have to love thee
> Does much excuse the appertaining rage
> To such a greeting: villain am I none;
> Therefore, farewell; I see thou know'st me not.

the riddle of it is plain only to us. Note that it is the old riddling Romeo that answers, but how changed! We can enjoy, too, the perplexity of those other onlookers and wonder if no one of them will jump to the meaning of the

> good Capulet, which name I tender
> As dearly as my own ...

But they stand stupent and Romeo passes on.

Upon each character concerned the situation tells differently; yet another test of its dramatic quality. Benvolio stands mute. He is all for peace, but such forbearance who can defend?[9] For Tybalt it is an all but comic letdown. The turning of the cheek makes the smiter look not brave, but ridiculous; and this 'courageous captain of compliments' takes ridicule very ill, is the readier, therefore, to recover his fire-eating dignity when Mercutio gives him the chance. And Mercutio, so doing, adds that most important ingredient to the situation, the unforeseen.

> Why the devil came you between us? [he gasps out to Romeo a short minute later] I was hurt under your arm.

But what the devil had he to do with a Capulet-Montague quarrel? The fact is (if one looks back) that he has been itching to read fashion-monger Tybalt a lesson; to show him that '*alla stoccata*' could not carry it away. But '*alla stoccata*' does; and, before we well know where we are, this arbitrary catastrophe gives the sharpest turn yet to the play's action, the liveliest of its figures crumples to impotence before us, the charming rhetoric of the Queen Mab speech has petered out in a savage growl.

The unexpected has its place in drama as well as the plotted and prepared. But observe that Shakespeare uses Mercutio's death to precipitate an essential change in Romeo; and it is this change, not anything extrinsic, that determines the main tragedy. After a parenthesis of scuffle and harsh prose he is left alone on the stage, and a simpler, graver, sterner emotion than any we have known in him yet begins to throb through measured verse.

> This gentleman, the Prince's near ally,
> My very friend, hath got this mortal hurt
> In my behalf; my reputation stained
> With Tybalt's slander—Tybalt, that an hour
> Hath been my cousin. O sweet Juliet,
> Thy beauty hath made me effeminate,
> And in my temper softened valour's steel!

Then he hears that his friend is dead, accepts his destiny—

> This day's black fate on more days doth depend;
> This but begins the woe others must end.

—and so to astonish the blood-intoxicated Tybalt! With a hundred words, but with expression and action transcending them, Shakespeare has tied the central knot of his play and brought his hero from height to depth.

We are sped on with little relaxation; returning, though, after these close-woven excitements, to declamation with Benvolio's diplomatic apologies (to the play's normal method, that is to say), while a second massed confronting of Montagues and Capulets marks, for reminder, this apex of the action.

We are sped on; and Juliet's ecstasy of expectation, the—

> Gallop apace, you fiery-footed steeds. . . .

—makes the best of contrasts, in matter and manner, to the sternness of Romeo's banishing. A yet sharper contrast follows quickly with the Nurse's coming, carrying the ladder of cords (the highway to the marriage bed, for emphasis of irony), standing mute a minute while Juliet stares, then breaking incontinently into her

> he's dead, he's dead, he's dead.

From now—with hardly a lapse to quiet—one scene will compete with the next in distraction till Friar Laurence comes to still the outcry of mourning over the drugged Juliet on her bed. The lovers compete in despair and desperate hope; Capulet precipitates confusion; the Friar himself turns foolhardy. All the action is shot through with haste and violence, and with one streak at least of gratuitous savagery besides. For if the plot demands Capulet's capricious tyrannies it does not need Lady Capulet's impulse to send a man after Romeo to poison him. But the freshly kindled virus of hatred (does Shakespeare feel?) must now spend itself even to exhaustion. From this point to the play's end, indeed, the one reposeful moment is when Romeo's

> dreams presage some joyful news at hand . . .

But the next is only the more shattering; and from then to the last tragic accidents it is a tale of yet worse violence, yet more reckless haste.[10]

It is, of course, in the end a tragedy of mischance. Shakespeare was bound by his story, was doubtless content to be; and how make it otherwise? Nevertheless, we discern his deeper dramatic sense, which was to shape the maturer tragedies, already in revolt. Accidents make good incidents, but tragedy determined by them has no significance. So he sets out, we see, in the shaping of his characters, to give all likelihood to the outcome. It is by pure ill-luck that Friar John's speed to Mantua is stayed while Balthasar reaches Romeo with the news of Juliet's death; but it is Romeo's headlong recklessness that leaves Friar Laurence no time to retrieve the mistake. It is, by a more subtle turn Juliet's overacted repentance of her 'disobedient opposition', which prompts the delighted Capulet to

> have this knot knit up to-morrow morning.

And this difference of a day proves also to be the difference between life and death.

Before ever the play begins, the chorus foretells its ending. The star-crossed lovers must, we are warned,

> with their death bury their parents' strife.

But Shakespeare is not content with the plain theme of an innocent happiness foredoomed. He makes good dramatic use of it. Our memory of the Prologue, echoing through the first scenes of happy encounter, lends them a poignancy which makes their beauties doubly beautiful. The sacrament of the marriage, with Romeo's invocation—

> Do thou but close our hands with holy words,
> Then love-devouring death do what he dare,
> It is enough I may but call her mine.

—read into it, stands as symbol of the sacrifice that all love and happiness must make to death. But character also is fate; it is, at any rate, the more dramatic part of it, and the life of Shakespeare's art is to lie in the manifesting of this. These two lovers, then, must in themselves be prone to disaster. They are never so freed from the accidents of their story as his later touch would probably have made them. But by the time he has brought them to their full dramatic stature we cannot—accidents or no—imagine a happy ending, or a Romeo and Juliet married and settled as anything but a burlesque.

So, the turning point of Mercutio's death and Tybalt's and Romeo's banishing being past, Shakespeare brings all his powers to bear upon the moulding of the two figures to inevitable tragedy; and the producer of the play must note with care how the thing is done. To begin with, over a succession of scenes—in all but one of which either Romeo or Juliet is concerned—there is no relaxing of tension, vehemence or speed; for every flagging moment in them there is some fresh spur, they reinforce each other too, the common practice of contrast between scene and scene is more or less foregone.[11] And the play's declamatory method is heightened, now into rhapsody, now into a veritable dervish-whirling of words.

Shakespeare's practical ability—while he still hesitates to discard it—to turn verbal conventions to lively account is shown to the full in the scene between Juliet and the Nurse, with which this stretch of the action begins—his success, also his failure. The passage in which Juliet's bewildered dread finds expression in a cascade of puns is almost invariably cut on the modern stage, and one may sympathize with the actress who shirks it. But it is, in fact, word-play perfectly adapted to dramatic use; and to the Elizabethans puns were not necessarily comic things.

> Hath Romeo slain himself? Say thou but 'I',
> And that bare vowel 'I' shall poison more
> Than the death-dealing eye of cockatrice:
> I am not I, if there be such an 'I',
> Or those eyes shut that make thee answer 'I'.
> If he be slain, say 'I'; or if not, no:
> Brief sounds determine of my weal or woe.

Shut our minds to its present absurdity (but it is no more absurd than any other bygone fashion), allow for the rhetorical method, and consider the emotional effect of the word-music alone—what a vivid expression of the girl's agonized mind it makes, this intoxicated confusion of words and meanings! The whole scene is written in terms of conventional rhetoric. We pass from play upon words to play upon phrase, paradox, antithesis.

> O serpent heart, hid with a flowering face!
> Did ever dragon keep so fair a cave?
> Beautiful tyrant; fiend angelical!
> Dove-feathered raven! wolfish ravening lamb!
> Despised substance of divinest show!
> Just opposite to what thou justly seem'st;
> A damned saint, an honourable villain! . . .

The boy-Juliet was here evidently expected to give a display of virtuosity comparable to the singing of a *scena* in a mid-nineteenth century opera. That there was no danger of the audience finding it ridiculous we may judge by Shakespeare's letting the Nurse burlesque the outcry with her

> There's no trust,
> No faith, no honesty in men; all perjured,
> All forsworn, all naught, all dissemblers!

For it is always a daring thing to sandwich farce with tragedy; and though Shakespeare was fond of doing it, obviously he would not if the tragedy itself were trembling on the edge of farce.

The weakness of the expedient shows later, when, after bringing us from rhetoric to pure drama with the Nurse's

> Will you speak well of him that killed your cousin?

and Juliet's flashing answer,

> Shall I speak ill of him that is my husband?

—one of those master touches that clarify and consummate a whole situation—Shakespeare must needs take us back to another screed of the sort which now shows meretricious by comparison. For a finish, though, we have the fine simplicity, set in formality, of

JULIET. Where is my father and my mother, Nurse?
NURSE. Weeping and wailing over Tybalt's corse:
  Will you go to them? I will bring you thither.
JULIET. Wash they his wounds with tears! Mine shall be spent,
  When theirs are dry, for Romeo's banishment.
  Take up those cords. Poor ropes, you are beguiled,
  Both you and I, for Romeo is exiled.
  He made you for a highway to my bed,
  But I, a maid, die maiden-widowed.

By one means and another, he has now given us a new and a passionate and desperate Juliet, more fitted to her tragic end.

In the scene that follows, we have desperate Romeo in place of desperate Juliet, with the Friar to lift it to dignity at the finish and to push the story a short step forward. The maturer Shakespeare would not, perhaps, have coupled such similar scenes so closely; but both likeness and repetition serve his present purpose.

To appraise the value of the next effect he makes we must again visualize the Elizabethan stage.[12] Below

Enter Capulet, Lady Capulet and Paris.

With Tybalt hardly buried, Juliet weeping for him, it has been no time for urging Paris' suit.

'Tis very late [says Capulet], she'll not come down to-night:
I promise you, but for your company,
I should have been a-bed an hour ago.

Paris takes his leave, asks Lady Capulet to commend him to her daughter. She answers him:

I will, and know her mind early to-morrow;
To-night she's mewed up to her heaviness.

But *we* know that, at this very moment, Romeo and Juliet, bride and bridegroom, are in each other's arms.
Paris is actually at the door, when, with a sudden impulse, Capulet recalls him.[13]

Sir Paris, I will make a desperate tender
Of my child's love. I think she will be ruled
In all respects by me; nay, more, I doubt it not.
Wife, go you to her ere you go to bed;
Acquaint her here of my son Paris' love,
And bid her, mark you me, on Wednesday next . . .

And by that sudden impulse, so lightly obeyed, the tragedy is precipitated. Capulet, bitten by an idea, is in a ferment.

Well, Wednesday is too soon;
O' Thursday let it be:—o' Thursday, tell her,
She shall be married to this noble earl.
Will you be ready? Do you like this haste? . . .

(In a trice he has shaken off the mourning uncle and turned jovial, roguish father-in-law.)

Well, get you gone! O' Thursday be it then.—
Go you to Juliet ere you go to bed,
Prepare her, wife, against this wedding day. . . .

(What, we are asking, will Lady Capulet find if she does
go?)

Farewell, my lord.—Light to my chamber, ho!
Afore me, it's so very late
That we may call it early by and by:—
Good-night.

Now comes the well-prepared effect. Hardly have the
three vanished below, bustling and happy; when with

Wilt thou begone? It is not yet near day. . . .

Juliet and Romeo appear at the window above, clinging
together, agonized in the very joy of their union, but all
ignorant of this new and deadly blow which (again) *we*
know is to fall on them.

Only the unlocalized stage is capable of just such an
effect as this. Delay in the shifting of scenery may be
overcome by the simple lifting of a front scene to
discover Romeo and Juliet in her chamber behind it;
but Shakespeare's audience had not even to shift their
imaginations from one place to another. The lower stage
was anywhere downstairs in Capulet's house. The upper
stage was associated with Juliet; it had served for her
balcony and had been put to no other use.[14] So while
Capulet is planning the marriage with Paris not only will
our thoughts have been travelling to her, but our eyes
may have rested speculatively, too, on those closed curtains above.

Shakespeare speeds his action all he can. Capulet,
itching with his new idea, gives invaluable help. Romeo
has hardly dropped from the balcony before Lady

Capulet is in her daughter's room.[15] Capulet himself comes on her heels. It is barely daybreak and he has not been to bed. (The night is given just that confused chronology such feverish nights seem to have.) With morning Juliet flies to the Friar, to find Paris already with him, the news already agitating him; she herself is the more agitated by the unlooked-for meeting with Paris. The encounter between them, with its equivoque, oddly echoes her first encounter with Romeo; but it is another Juliet that now plays a suitor with words. It is a more deeply passionate Juliet, too, that turns from Paris' formal kiss with

> Oh, shut the door, and when thou hast done so,
> Come weep with me; past hope, past cure, past help!

than so passionately greeted the news of Tybalt's death and Romeo's banishment. Child she may still be, but she is now a wife.

We should count the Friar's long speech with which he gives her the potion, in which he tells her his plan, as a sort of strong pillar of rhetoric, from which the play's action is to be swung to the next strong pillar, the speech (in some ways its counterpart) in which Juliet nerves herself to the drinking it. For, with Romeo removed for the moment, the alternating scene falls to Capulet and his bustlings; these are admirable as contrast, but of no dramatic power, and the action at this juncture must be well braced and sustained.

We come now to another and still more important effect, that is (yet again) only to be realized in the theatre for which it was designed. The curtains of the inner stage are drawn back to show us Juliet's bed. Her nurse and her mother leave her; she drinks the potion, and—says that note-taker at the performance, whose business it was, presumably, to let his employers know exactly how all the doubtful bits were done—

She falls upon the bed within the curtains.

There has been argument upon argument whether this means the curtains of the bed or of the inner stage— which would then close on her. The difference in dramatic effect will be of degree and not kind. What Shakespeare aims at in the episodes that follow is to keep us conscious of the bed and its burden; while in front of it, Capulet and the servants, Lady Capulet and the Nurse pass hither and thither, laughing and joking over the preparation for the wedding, till the bridal music is playing, till, to the very sound of this, the Nurse bustles up to draw back the curtains and disclose the girl there stark and still.[16]

This is one of the chief dramatic effects of the play; and it can only be gained by preserving the continuity of the action, with its agonies and absurdities cheek by jowl, with that bridal music sharpening the irony at the last. It is a comprehensive effect, extending from the drinking of the potion to the Nurse's parrot scream when she finds Juliet stiff and cold; and even beyond, to the coming of the bridegroom and his train, through the long-spoken threnody, to the farce of the ending—which helps to remind us that, after all, Juliet is not dead. It is one scene, one integral stretch of action; and its common mutilation by *Scene iv. Hall in Capulet's house . . . Scene v. Juliet's chamber. Enter Nurse . . .* , with the consequences involved, is sheer editorial murder.

Modern producers, as a rule, do even worse by it than the editors. They bring down a curtain upon a display of virtuosity in a 'potion-scene', long drawn out, worried to bits, and leave us to recover till they are ready with Romeo in Mantua and the apothecary. And even faithful

Shakespeareans have little good to say of that competition in mourning between Paris and Capulet, Lady Capulet and the Nurse. It has been branded as deliberate burlesque. It is assuredly no more so than was Juliet's outbreak against Romeo upon Tybalt's death; to each, we notice, the Nurse provides a comic, characteristic echo, which would have little point if it did not contrast, rather absurdly, with the rest. Burlesque, of a sort, comes later with Peter and the musicians; Shakespeare would not anticipate this effect, and so equivocally! The passage does jar a little; but we must remember that he is working here in a convention that has gone somewhat stale with him, and constrainedly; and that he can call now on no such youthful, extravagant passion as Juliet's or Romeo's to make the set phrases live. The situation is dramatically awkward, besides; in itself it mocks at the mourners, and Friar Laurence's reproof of them, which comes unhappily near to cant, hardly clarifies it. Shakespeare comes lamely out; but he went sincerely in. Nor does the farce of Peter and the musicians, conventional as it is, stray wholly beyond likelihood. Peter is comic in his grief; but many people are. Will Kempe, it may be, had to have his fling; but this part of the scene has its dramatic value, too. It develops and broadens—vulgarizes, if you will—the irony of the bridal music brought to the deathbed; and, the traditional riddle-me-ree business done with (and Will Kempe having 'brought off an exit' amid cheers), there is true sting in the tail of it:

FIRST MUSICIAN.   What a pestilent knave is this same!
SECOND MUSICIAN. Hang him, Jack! Come, we'll in here;
  tarry for the mourners, and stay dinner.

And, of course, it eases the strain before tragedy gets its final grip of us.

We find Romeo in Mantua poised upon happiness before his last sudden plunge to despair and death. Shakespeare has now achieved simplicity in his treatment of him, brought the character to maturity and his own present method to something like perfection. What can be simpler, more obvious yet more effective than the dream with its flattering presage of good news—

> I dreamt my lady came and found me dead—
> Strange dream, that gives a dead man leave to think!—
> And breathed such life with kisses in my lips,
> That I revived, and was an emperor. . . .

—followed incontinently by Balthasar's

> Her body sleeps in Capels' monument,
> And her immortal part with angels lives. . . .

So much for dreams! So much for life and its flatteries! And the buying of the poison shows us a Romeo grown out of all knowledge away from the sentimental, phrase-making adorer of Rosaline.

> There is thy gold; worse poison to men's souls,
> Doing more murder in this loathsome world
> Than these poor compounds that thou mayst not sell:
> I sell thee poison, thou hast sold me none.

This ageing of Romeo is marked by more than one touch. To the contemptuous Tybalt he was a boy; now Paris to him, when they meet, is to be 'good gentle youth'.

Then, after one more needed link in the story has been riveted, we reach the play's last scene. Producers are accustomed to eliminate most of this, keeping the slaughtering of Paris as a prelude, concentrating upon Romeo's death and Juliet's, possibly providing a sort of symbolic picture of Montagues and Capulets reconciled

at the end. This is all very well, and saves us the sweet
kernel of the nut, no doubt; but it happens not to be
the scene that Shakespeare devised. To appreciate that
we must once more visualize the stage for which it was
devised. The authorities are in dispute upon several
points here, but only of detail. Juliet lies entombed in
the inner stage; that is clear. The outer stage stands for
the churchyard; as elastically as it stood before for the
street or the courtyard of Capulet's house in which the
Maskers marched about, while the serving-men coming
forth with their napkins converted it, as vaguely, into the
hall. Now it is as near to the tomb or as far from it as
need be, and the action on it (it is the larger part of this
that is usually cut) will be prominent and important. The
tomb itself is the inner stage, closed in, presumably, by
gates which Romeo breaks open, through the bars of
which Paris casts his flowers. Juliet herself lies like a
recumbent effigy upon a rectangular block of stone,
which must be low enough and wide enough for Romeo
to lie more or less beside her; and other such monu-
ments, uneffigied, Tybalt's among them, may surround
her.[17]

Once more Shakespeare hurries us through a whole
night of confusion; from the coming of Paris, the cheated
bridegroom, and Romeo, the robbed husband, to this
ghastly bride-bed, through one tragic miscarrying after
another, to the Prince's summing-up:

A glooming peace this morning with it brings. . . .

All is confusion; only the regularity of the verse keeps it
from running away. Paris is fearful of disturbance,[18] and
Romeo, when he comes, is strained beyond endurance
or control. It is not till he has fleshed the edge of his
desperation upon poor Paris, till he is sobered by seeing
what he has done, that, armed securely with his poison,

he can take his calm farewell. Once he is dead, confusion is let loose. The Friar approaches with

> Saint Francis be my speed! How oft to-night
> Have my old feet stumbled at graves! . . .

Balthasar and he whisper and tremble. Then Juliet wakes; but before he can speak to her, the watch are heard coming. He flies; and she has but time to find the empty phial in Romeo's hand, bare time to find his dagger and stab herself before they appear, and the hunt is up:

PARIS' PAGE. This is the place; there, where the torch doth burn.
CAPTAIN OF The ground is bloody; search about the
THE WATCH.   churchyard:
  Go, some of you, whoe'er you find, attach.
  Pitiful sight! here lies the county slain,
  And Juliet bleeding, warm and newly dead,
  Who here hath lain this two days buried.[19]
  Go, tell the Prince; run to the Capulets;
  Raise up the Montagues; some others search. . . .

Cries, confusion, bustle; some of the watch bring back Balthasar, some others the Friar; the Prince arrives with his train, the Capulets surge in, the Montagues; the whole front stage is filled with the coming and going, while, in dreadful contrast, plain to our sight within the tomb, the torchlight flickering on them, Romeo and Juliet lie still.[20]

    The play is not over, another hundred lines go to its finishing; and, to appease our modern impatience of talk when no more is to be done, here, if nowhere else, the producer will wield the blue pencil doughtily. Why should the Friar recount at length—after saying he'll be brief, moreover!—what we already know, with Balthasar to follow suit, and Paris' page to follow him? There are half a dozen good reasons. Shakespeare neither could nor would, of course, bring a play to a merely catastrophic end; the traditions of his stage no less than its conditions forbade this. Therefore the Prince's authoritative

> Seal up the mouth of outrage for a while,
> Till we can clear these ambiguities,
> And know their spring, their head, their true descent;
> And then I will be general of your woes,
> And lead you even to death: meantime forbear....

with which he stills a tumult that threatens otherwise to end the play, as it began, in bloody rough-and-tumble— this is the obvious first note of a formal full-close. But the Friar's story must be told, because the play's true end is less in the death of the star-crossed lovers than in the burying of their parents' strife; and as it has been primarily a play of tangled mischances, the unravelling of these, the bringing home of their meaning to the sufferers by them, is a natural part of its process. How else lead up to the Prince's

> Where be these enemies? Capulet—Montague!
> See what a scourge is laid upon your hate....

and to the solution with Capulet's

> O brother Montague, give me thy hand....

For us also—despite our privileged vision—it has been a play of confused, passion-distorted happenings, and the Friar's plain tale makes the simple pity of them clear, and sends us away with this foremost in our minds. Again, declamation is the norm of the play's method, and it is natural to return to that for a finish. Finally, as it is a tragedy less of character than of circumstance, upon circumstance its last emphasis naturally falls. Yet, all this admitted, one must own that the penultimate stretch of the writing, at least, is poor in quality. Shakespeare has done well by his story and peopled it with passionate life. But, his impulse flagging, his artistry is still found immature. Compare the poverty of this ending with the resourceful breadth of the effect made in the rounding of the story of *Cymbeline* to a close.

The Question of Act-Division

NEITHER Quartos nor Folio mark act-division; Rowe first supplies it, and his arrangement has commonly been accepted since. There are several questions involved. Did Shakespeare plan out the play as an indivisible whole? If he did, was it so acted; and, if not, were the pauses made mere formal pauses, or intervals, in which the emotional tension would not only relax, but lapse altogether? And, pauses or intervals, is Rowe's placing of them authentic? With the historical aspect of all this I am incompetent to deal. But Rowe's dividing-up of the action is, clearly, neither here nor there; and even if it is not his, but a somehow inherited tradition, that still will not make it Shakespeare's. A play, as we know, soon passed beyond its author's control, and Elizabethan practice may have differed from play to play, and as between the public theatre and the private. How did Shakespeare *plan* his play? That is what we have to divine if we can; and from that we may pass directly to the question of our own convenience in the acting of it.

The one internal piece of evidence of a lost scheme of act-division is the second chorus. This, incidentally, does not appear in the first Quarto. Is it capable of any other explanation? It has little dramatic point, as to this Johnson's robust verdict suffices; ' . . . it conduces nothing to the progress of the play, but relates what is already known, or what the next scene will show; and relates it without adding the improvement of any moral sentiment'. It has been held very doubtfully Shakespearean. There is one thing to note about it and the scene which precedes it. This requires stools to be set on the outer stage for the use of Capulet and his cousin. They are presumably the joint-stools of the text, and the text makes provision for their setting. But we find none for their taking-away, no dialogue to help out the business, and they could not well be moved during the latter half of the scene, when Romeo and Juliet are love-making. In an act-pause they could presumably have been moved; but if there were none—was the chorus by chance written in to cover this technical clumsiness? It is possible; but the remedy seems as clumsy as the fault.[21]

Later, Shakespeare lands himself in a more serious technical difficulty, from which, though at some sacrifice of dramatic effect, an act-pause would have extricated him. He wants to show us Romeo and Juliet parting on their wedding night, Romeo descending from the very balcony which had seen their wooing and their brief happiness, and to follow this quickly by the bringing of the news to Juliet that she is to marry Paris. The double blow, no respite given, was the important thing to him dramatically, without doubt. But would he not have saved himself, if he well could, from the present ensuing clumsiness that brings Juliet from upper stage to lower in the middle of a scene, her bedroom on her back, as it were? Though an Elizabethan audience might make light of a lapse of this sort, it is none the less clumsy, and from the beginning he was an apt if a daring craftsman.[22]

Lastly, was the scene between Peter and the musicians written for its own sake, or to please Will Kempe, or (possibly) to make more time than the two scenes which carry on the plot allow for the moving of the bed and the setting of the tomb upon the inner stage?[23] If Rowe's act-pause had intervened there would have been time enough. These are trivial matters, but not wholly negligible.

If five acts there must be, Rowe's five may serve. But one could vary the division as legitimately in half a dozen different ways; and this in itself argues against any division at all. Nor is there any scene-division in the play, where an act-division might fall, over which some immediate bridge does not seem to be thrown. Either a strong contrast is devised between the end of one scene and the beginning of the next that a pause would nullify, or the quick succession of event to event is an integral part of the dramatic effect Shakespeare is seeking. (But it is, of course, in the very nature of the play, of its precipitate passion, to forge ahead without pause.) What value is there in an act-pause after Capulet's supper, between Romeo's first meeting with Juliet and the bal-cony-scene? There is no interval of time to account for, nor has the action reached any juncture that asks for the emphasis of a pause. An act-pause after the marriage falls with a certain effect, but it nullifies the far better effect by which Tybalt is shown striding the streets in search of Romeo at the very moment when the Friar is marrying him to Juliet; and that Romeo should seem to come straight from the marriage to face Tybalt's chal-lenge is a vital dramatic point. The whole action surges to a crisis with the deaths of Tybalt and Mercutio and Romeo's banishing; and here, one could argue, a pause while we asked, 'What next?' might have its value. But Rowe marks no act-pause here; and if he did, the fine effect by which Juliet's ecstatic

Gallop apace, you fiery-footed steeds. . . .

follows pat upon the Prince's

> let Romeo hence in haste,
> Else, when he's found, that hour is his last.

would be destroyed. The break made between Juliet's
departure to the Friar's cell for counsel how to escape
the marriage with Paris and her arrival there and the
encounter with him relates to no pause, nor check,
nor turn in the action. Rowe's Act IV, we may say,
then begins with the new interest of the giving of the
potion, as it ends upon an echo of its taking. And
a pause—a breathing-space before the great plunge
into tragedy—before we find Romeo in Mantua waiting for news (before Rowe's Act V, that is to say) may
have dramatic value. But the comic scene with the
musicians provides just such a breathing-space. And if
we remove it (and there may have been, as I suggest,
merely incidental reasons for putting it in) a continuity
of action is restored which gives us a most dramatic
contrast between the mourning over Juliet and Romeo's
buoyant hopes.

What we should look for, surely, in act-division, is
some definite advantage to the play's acting. Where, in
this play, do we find that? But the gains are patent if
we act it without check or pause. Whatever the Elizabethan practice may have been, and whatever concessions
are to be made to pure convenience, everything seems
to point to Shakespeare having *planned* the play as a thing
indivisible. It can be so acted without much outrunning
the two hours' traffic.[24] If this will overtax the weakness
of the flesh—the audience's; for actors will profit by the
unchecked flow of action and emotion—some sacrifice
of effect must be made. The less then, the better. A
single pause after the banishing of Romeo would be my
own solution.

Staging, Costume, Music, Text

THE producer wishing to enscene the play must devise such scenery as will not deform, obscure or prejudice its craftsmanship or its art. That is all. But it is not easy to do.

There are no signs in the text that Shakespeare saw Italian touches added to the players' normal costumes. Italian costumes will serve, as long as rapier and dagger go with them, and may add something to the effect of the play upon us; but Elizabethan doublet and hose will take next to nothing of it away.

The text tells us pretty plainly what music is needed. It is a consort of recorders that Paris brings with him to the wedding; and the musicians either enter with him, playing, to be stopped incontinently by the sight of the tragic group round the bed; or (this is, I think, more likely) they stay playing the bridal music without, a tragically ironical accompaniment to the lamenting over Juliet, till they are stopped and come clustering—scared, incongruous figures—into the doorway.[25]

> Faith, we may put up our pipes and be gone.

says the leader, when the mourners depart (all but the Nurse, who needs a line or two to speak while she draws the inner-stage curtains), leaving them alone.

The recorders could play for the dance at Capulet's too. But a consort of viols is perhaps likelier here, for there is dialogue throughout the music, and one does not speak through wood-wind with impunity. The musicians probably sat in their gallery.

The text itself raises many minor questions that need not be dealt with here. But no one should omit to read the first Quarto. For all its corruptions, it gives us now and then a vivid picture of a performance Shakespeare himself must presumably have supervised. It may not be much to know that Juliet entered *somewhat fast* and embraced Romeo[26]; that when Romeo *offers to stab himself* the Nurse *snatches the dagger away*; that (but this point we have remarked as important) at one juncture *Paris offers to goe in and Capolet calls him againe*; that they cast rosemary on the Juliet they think dead; and that Paris comes with his page to the tomb bringing flowers and *sweete water* with him too. But Shakespeare's stage directions are rarities indeed; and these and other such small touches give life to the rudimentary text, and an actuality to the play that scrupulous editing seems, somehow, to reform altogether.

Not but that the text has needed editing enough; and there are puzzles, such as the notorious 'runaway's eyes' (twenty-eight pages devoted to it in the Furness Variorum!), yet unsolved. But few, if any, of them are of dramatic moment; and there is amply varied authority to bow to. The producer has his own few problems to face. There is the minor one of indecency. One or two of Mercutio's jokes are too outrageous for modern public usage; they will create discomfort among a mixed audience instead of laughter. But this full-blooded sensuality is (as we have seen) set very purposefully against Romeo's romantic idealism, and the balance and contrast must not be destroyed. A Mercutio who lets his mouth be stopped by a prim Benvolio each time he launches on a smutty joke will be a cowed, a 'calm, dishonourable, vile' Mercutio indeed.

But a producer is tempted to far more cutting than this, and most producers fall. The play as commonly presented to us starts fairly true to Shakespeare, a troublesome passage suppressed here and there; but, as it advances, more and more of the text disappears, till the going becomes hop-skip-and-jump, and 'Selections from the tragedy of Romeo and Juliet' would be a truer title for it. This will not do. The construction, very naturally, does not show the skill of Shakespeare's maturity, nor does every character stand consistent and foursquare; the writing runs to extravagant rhetoric and often to redundancy. But his chosen method of close consecutive narrative will be lamed by mutilation; and rhetoric and redundancy, the violence, the absurdities even, are the medium in which the characters are quite intentionally painted. To omit the final scurry of Montagues and Capulets and citizens of Verona to the tomb and the Friar's redundant story for the sake of finishing upon the more poignant note of Juliet's death is, as we have seen, to falsify Shakespeare's whole intention; and to omit the sequel to the drinking of the potion is as bad and worse! Restoring the play to its own sort of stage will serve to curb these follies, at least.

The verbiage and its eccentricities—as they sound to our modern incurious ears—seem, at first blush, harder to compass. No producer need be pedantic; it is his business to gain an effect, not to prejudice it. But much that strikes one as strange in print, that may jar under the repetition and cold-blooded analysis of rehearsals, will pass and make its own effect in the rush of performance. The cutting of a speech or two from a scene is like the removal of a few bricks from a wall; it may be a harmless operation and it may not. The structure may stand up as strongly with the hole in it, or it may sag, or come tumbling altogether. The antiphonal mourning over Juliet is crude, doubtless, and one is tempted to get rid of it, or at least to modify it. Do so, and what becomes of the calming effect of Friar Laurence's long speeches? There will be nothing for him to calm. Cut this too, and Capulet will have to turn without rhyme or reason from distracted grief to dignified resignation,

while the others, the Friar included, stand like foolish
lay figures.

To protest against the omission of the—to us—incongruous pun which bisects Romeo's passionate outburst,
his

> This may flies do, when I from this must fly. . . .

would be pedantry. The play will not be the worse for
its loss; the only question is whether it is worth omitting.
But to shirk Juliet's delirium of puns upon 'Ay' and 'I'
and 'eye' is to lower the scene's temperature and flatten
it out when Shakespeare has planned to lift it, by these
very means, to a sudden height of intoxicated excite-
ment, giving us a first and memorable taste of the Juliet
of quick despair, who later, in a flash of resolution, will
sheath Romeo's dagger in her heart.

There is no more dangerous weapon than the blue
pencil.

The Characters

THIS is a tragedy of youth, as youth sees it, and age is
not let play a very distinguished part. Friar Laurence is
sympathetic, but he is compact of maxims, of pedagogic
kindness; he is just such a picture of an old man as a
young man draws, all unavailing wisdom. There is no
more life in the character than the story asks and gives;
but Shakespeare palliates this dramatic weakness by
keeping him shadowed in his cell, a ghostly confessor, a
refuge for Romeo, Paris and Juliet alike, existing—as in
their youthful egoism we may be sure they thought—in
their interests alone.

It is noteworthy what an arbitrary line is drawn between youth and age; arbitrary, but at times uncertain.

Capulet and Montague are conventionally 'old', though their children are young enough for them not to have passed forty. Capulet gives some excuse for this by saying of Juliet that

> The earth hath swallowed all my hopes but she. . . .

So we may surmise, if we will, a cluster of sons killed in the vendetta, or that sad little Elizabethan procession of infant effigies to be carved in time on his tomb. But Lady Capulet passes from saying that she was but fourteen herself at Juliet's birth fourteen years ago to telling us in the end that

> This sight of death is as a bell
> That warns my old age to a sepulchre.[27]

And the Nurse is old, though not fourteen years ago she had a child of her own and was suckling Juliet. It is futile trying to resolve these anomalies. Shakespeare wants a sharp conflict set between youth and age; he emphasizes every aspect of it, and treats time of life much as he treats time of day—for effect.

THE NURSE

The Nurse, whatever her age, is a triumphant and complete achievement. She stands foursquare, and lives and breathes in her own right from the moment she appears, from that very first

> Now, by my maidenhead at twelve year old,
> I bade her come.

Shakespeare has had her pent up in his imagination; and out she gushes. He will give us nothing completer till he gives us Falstaff. We mark his confident, delighted knowledge of her by the prompt digression into which he lets her launch; the story may wait. It is not a set piece of fireworks such as Mercutio will touch off in honour of Queen Mab. The matter of it flows spontaneously into verse, the phrases are hers and hers alone, character unfolds with each phrase. You may, indeed, take any sentence the Nurse speaks throughout the play, and only she could speak it. Moreover, it will have no trace of the convention to which Shakespeare himself is still tied (into which he forces, to some extent, every other character), unless we find her burlesquing it. But the good Angelica—which we at last discover to be her perfect name—needs no critical expanding, she expounds herself on all occasions; nor explanation, for she is plain as daylight; nor analysis, lest it lead to excuse; and she stays blissfully unregenerate. No one can fail to act her well that can speak her lines. Yet they are so supercharged with life that they will accommodate the larger acting—which is the revelation of a personality in terms of a part—and to the full; and it may be as rich a personality as can be found. She is in everything inevitable; from her

My fan, Peter.

when she means to play the discreet lady with those gay young sparks, to that all unexpected

Faith, here 'tis; Romeo
Is banished; and all the world to nothing,
That he dares ne'er come back to challenge you;
Or if he do, it needs must be by stealth.
Then, since the case so stands as now it doth,
I think it best you married with the county.

—horrifyingly unexpected to Juliet; but to us, the moment she has said it, the inevitable thing for her to say.

This last turn, that seems so casually made, is the stroke that completes the character. Till now we have taken her—the 'good, sweet Nurse'—just as casually, amused by each comicality as it came; for so we do take the folk that amuse us. But with this everything about her falls into perspective, her funniments, her endearments, her grossness, her good nature; upon the instant, they all find their places in the finished picture. And for a last enrichment, candidly welling from the lewd soul of her, comes

> O, he's a lovely gentleman;
> Romeo's a dishclout to him; an eagle, Madam,
> Hath not so green, so quick, so fair an eye
> As Paris hath. Beshrew my very heart,
> I think you are happy in this second match,
> For it excels your first; or if it did not,
> Your first is dead, or 'twere as good he were
> As living hence and you no use of him.

Weigh the effect made upon Juliet, fresh from the sacrament of love and the bitterness of parting, by the last fifteen words of that.

> Speak'st thou from thy heart?
>
>   And from my soul too,
> Or else beshrew them both.
>
>   Amen!

It is gathered into the full-fraught 'Amen'. But best of all, perhaps, is the old bawd's utter unconsciousness of having said anything out of the way. And when she finds her lamb, her ladybird, returning from shrift with merry look—too merry!—how should she suppose she has not given her the wholesomest advice in the world?

We see her obliviously bustling through the night's preparations for this new wedding. We hear her—incredibly!—start to stir Juliet from her sleep with the same

coarse wit that had served to deepen the girl's blushes
for Romeo's coming near. We leave her blubbering
grotesquely over the body she had been happy to deliver
to a baser martyrdom. Shakespeare lets her pass from
the play without comment. Is any needed?[28]

CAPULET

Capulet, again, is a young man's old man. But he is
more opulently done than the Friar, if he has not the flesh,
blood, bones and all of the good Angelica. He suffers more
than any other character in the play by its customary
mutilations; for these leave him a mere domestic tyrant,
and Shakespeare does not. With his benevolent airs,
self-conscious hilarity, childish ill-temper, he is that yet
commoner type, the petted and spoiled husband and
father and head of the house; and the study of him
might be more effective if it were not strung out through
the play, and so intermittently touched in. But he is
planned consistently—with all his inconsistencies—from
the beginning.

The flavour of gratified vanity in

> But Montague is bound as well as I
> In penalty alike . . .

puts us at once upon easy terms with him. And Shakespeare hardly wrote,

> But woo her, gentle Paris, get her heart,
> My will to her consent is but a part. . . .

without having

> An you be mine, I'll give you to my friend;
> An you be not, hang, beg, starve, die in the streets. . . .

in his mind already. Our next sight of him gives us the
breeze with Tybalt, the chop and change of

> Well said, my hearts! You are a princox; go:
> Be quiet, or—More light, more light!—For shame!
> I'll make you quiet.—What, cheerly, my hearts!

This is Capulet at home, a familiar figure in many a
home; the complete gentleman, the genial host, the
kindliest of men—as long as no one crosses him.

Old as he is, he was ready enough to take part in
the earlier brawl; but we note that he stands silent
before Tybalt's body, and Lady Capulet is left to cry out
for revenge. He did not the less love Tybalt dearly
because he can turn promptly from the thought of him
to Juliet's marriage to Paris, and change his decorous
resolve to

> keep no great ado; a friend or two;
> For, hark you, Tybalt being slain so late,
> It may be thought we held him carelessly,
> Being our kinsman, if we revel much.

into

> Sirrah, go hire me twenty cunning cooks.

He is incorrigibly hospitable, that is one thing. For
another, it is obviously a wise move, Capulets and
Montagues both being now in worse odour than ever in
Verona, to marry Juliet as soon as may be to this
kinsman of the Prince. And except for the haste of it
(nor would even that greatly astonish them) his

> Sir Paris, I will make a desperate tender
> Of my child's love. I think she will be ruled
> In all respects by me; nay, more, I doubt it not.

would not seem to an Elizabethan audience very un-
usual. His vituperative raging against the obstinate girl
does bring his wife and the Nurse to her rescue.

> Out, you green-sickness carrion! out, you baggage!
> You tallow face!

—moves even Lady Capulet to protest. But he is merely
raging; and parents of the day, finding their fingers itch
to chastise young ladies of riper years than Juliet, did
not always let them itch in vain. For a thrashing then
and there ample precedent could be cited. And an hour
or two later he is quite good-tempered again.

> How now, my headstrong! where have you been gadding?

he hails her.

He is not insincere, as he is not undignified, in his
heartbroken outcry at her supposed death, if we may
divine Shakespeare's intention through a crudely written
scene. And he stands, dignified and magnanimous in his
sorrow, at the last. It is a partial picture of a man, no
doubt, ill-emphasized at times, and at times crippled by
convention; but of a most recognizable man, and never
untrue. Note lastly that it is the portrait of a very English
old gentleman.[29] When did the phlegmatic Englishman—
or the legend of him—come into fashion as the type of
his kind?

THE MINOR CHARACTERS; AND MERCUTIO

The play has its full share of merely conventional
figures, from the Prince to Peter, Abram and his fellows,
to Balthasar and Paris' page; and they must be treated
for what they are. Lady Capulet is sketchily uncertain.
Benvolio is negative enough, confidant to Romeo, foil
to Mercutio. But there are such men; and Shakespeare
endows him with a kindly patience, sharpens his wit
every now and again to a mild irony, gives him a steady
consistency that rounds him to something more than a
shadow.

Tybalt we must see somewhat through Mercutio's eyes. Pretty obviously we are meant to; and the actor must take the hint, nor make him a mere blusterer, but something at least of a

> courageous captain of compliments ... the very butcher of a silk button, a duellist, a duellist; a gentleman of the very first house, of the first and second cause.

He need not, however, place him irretrievably among the

> antic, lisping, affecting fantasticoes, these new tuners of accents ... these fashion-mongers, these *pardonnez-mois* ...

He may reasonably discount a little Mercutio's John Bull prejudices.

For Mercutio, when Shakespeare finally makes up his mind about him, is in temperament very much the young John Bull of his time; and as different from the stocky, stolid John Bull of our later picturing as Capulet from the conventional heavy father. There can be, of course, no epitomizing of a race in any one figure. But the dominant qualities of an age are apt to be set in a pattern, which will last in literature, though outmoded, till another replaces it.

We learn little about Mercutio as he goes racketing to Capulet's supper, except that John Bull is often a poetic sort of fellow, or as he returns, unless it be that a man may like smut and fairy tales too. But he is still in the toils of conventional versifying, and a victim besides, probably, to his author's uncertainty about him. The authentic Mercutio only springs into life with

> Where the devil should this Romeo be? Came he not home to-night?

when he springs to life indeed. From now on he abounds in his own sense, and we can put him to the test the

Nurse abides by; not a thing that he says could anyone else say. He asks as little exposition, he is what he is with perfect clarity; the more so probably because he is wholly Shakespeare's creation, his namesake in Brooke's poem giving no hint of him. And (as with the Nurse) we could transport this authentic Mercutio into the maturest of the plays and he would fall into place there, nor would he be out of place on any stage, in any fiction.

A wholesome self-sufficiency is his cardinal quality; so he suitably finds place among neither Capulets nor Montagues. Shakespeare endows him, we saw, with a jolly sensuality for a setoff to Romeo's romancings; and, by a later, significant touch, adds to the contrast. When their battle of wits is ending—a breathless bandying of words that is like a sharp set at tennis—suddenly, it would seem, he throws an affectionate arm round the younger man's shoulder.[30]

> Why, is not this better now than groaning for love? Now art thou sociable, now art thou Romeo, now art thou what thou art. . . .

Mercutio's creed in a careless sentence! At all costs be the thing you are. The more his—and the more John Bullish—that we find it dropped casually amid a whirl of chaff and never touched on again! Here is the man. No wistful ideals for him; but life as it comes and death when it comes. A man of soundest common sense surely; the complete realist, the egoist justified. But by the day's end he has gone to his death in a cause not his own, upon pure impulse and something very like principle. There is no inconsistency in this; such vital natures must range between extremes.

> Rightly to be great
> Is not to stir without great argument,

> But greatly to find quarrel in a straw,
> When honour's at the stake.

That is a later voice, troublously questioning. Mercutio
pretends neither to greatness nor philosophy. When the
moment comes, it is not his own honour that is at stake;
but such calm, dishonourable, vile submission is more
than flesh and blood can bear. That the Mercutios of
the world quarrel on principle they would hate to be
told. Quarrel with a man for cracking nuts, having no
other reason but because one has hazel eyes; quarrel,
with your life in your hand, for quarrelling's sake, since
quarrelling and fighting are a part of life, and the
appetite for them human nature. Mercutio fights Tybalt
because he feels he must, because he cannot stand the
fellow's airs a moment longer. He'll put him in his place,
if no one else will. He fights without malice, not in anger
even, and for no advantage. He fights because he is what
he is, to testify to this simple unconscious faith, and goes
in with good honest cut and thrust. But *alla stoccata*
carries it away; and he, the perfect realist, the egoist
complete, dies for an ideal. Extremes have met.

No regrets though; nor any hypocrisy of resignation
for him! He has been beaten by the thing he despised,
and is as robustly angry about it as if he had years to
live in which to get his own back.

> Zounds! a dog, a rat, a mouse, a cat, to scratch a man to
> death! A braggart, a rogue, a villain, that fights by the book
> of arithmetic!

He is brutally downright with Romeo:

> Why the devil came you between us? I was hurt under
> your arm.[31]

and, after that, says no more to him, ignores the pitifully
futile

I thought all for the best.

dies with his teeth set, impenitently himself to the last.

ROMEO

We have Romeo and Juliet themselves left to consider; the boy and girl—they are no more—caught with their love as in a vice between the hatreds of their houses, to be crushed to death there.

Romeo has been called an early study for Hamlet. It is true enough to be misleading. The many ideas that go to make up Hamlet will have seeded themselves from time to time in Shakespeare's imagination, sprouting a little, their full fruition delayed till the dominant idea ripened. We can find traits of Hamlet in Romeo, in Richard II, in Jaques, in less likely habitations. But Romeo is not a younger Hamlet in love, though Hamlet in love may seem a disillusioned Romeo. The very likeness, moreover, is largely superficial, is a common likeness to many young men, who take life desperately seriously, some with reason, some without. The study of him is not plain sailing. If Hamlet's melancholy is of the soul, Romeo's was something of a pose; and there is Shakespeare's own present convention to account for, of word-spinning and thought-spinning, in which he cast much of the play, through which he broke more and more while he wrote it; there are, besides, the abundant remains of Brooke's Romeus. Romeo is in the making till the end; and he is made by fits and starts. Significant moments reveal him; but, looking back, one perceives screeds of the inessential, more heat than light in them. The actor's first task will be to distinguish between the significant and the passingly effective, and his last, as he plays the part, to adjust and reconcile the two.

Decorative method allowed for, the Romeo of

Why then, O brawling love! O loving hate!
O anything, of nothing first create!
O heavy lightness! serious vanity!
Misshapen chaos of well-seeming forms!
Feather of lead, bright smoke, cold fire, sick health!
Still-waking sleep, that is not what it is! . . .

pictures an actual Romeo truly enough; and, if it seems
to overcolour him, why, this Romeo was busy at the
moment overcolouring himself. Yet amid all the phrase-
mongering we may detect a phrase or two telling of a
deeper misprision than the obduracy of Rosaline ac-
counts for. The inconsequent

Show me a mistress that is passing fair,
What doth her beauty serve but as a note
Where I may read who passed that passing fair?

is very boyish cynicism, but it marks the unhappy nature.
And Rosaline herself was a Capulet, it seems (in that
camp, at any rate); so, had she smiled on him, his stars
would still have been crossed. He is posing to himself
certainly, more in love with love than with Rosaline,
posing to his family and friends, and not at all displeased
by their concern. But beneath all this, the mind that, as
he passes with the Maskers and their festive drum to
Capulet's feast,

misgives
Some consequence, yet hanging in the stars . . .

shows the peculiar clarity which gives quality to a man,
marks him off from the happy-go-lucky crowd, and will
at a crisis compel him to face his fate. By a few touches,
then, and in a melody of speech that is all his own, he
is set before us, a tragic figure from the first.

He sees Juliet. Shakespeare insists on the youth of the
two, and more than once on their innocence, their

purity—his as well as hers. It is not purposelessly that he is given the Dian-like Rosaline for a first love; nor that his first words to Juliet, as he touches her finger tips, are

> If I profane with my unworthiest hand
> This holy shrine . . .

nor that their first exchange is in the pretty formality of a sonnet, the kiss with which it ends half jest, half sacrament.[32] But their fate is sealed by it, there and then. They cannot speak again, for Lady Capulet calls Juliet away; and Benvolio, ever cautious, urges Romeo out of danger before there may be question of unmasking and discovery. Not before he has accepted his fate, though, and she hers—for better, for worse, without doubt, question, or hesitation! He (if we are to note niceties) accepts it even more unquestioningly than she. But her cry when she first hears his name gives us early promise of the rebellious Juliet, the more reckless and desperate of the two.

They look into the abyss and then give no more heed to it. Virginal passion sweeps them aloft and away, and to its natural goal. What should hinder? Nothing in themselves, none of the misgiving that experience brings; and for counsellors they have Nurse and Friar, she conscienceless, he as little worldly as they. Juliet is no questioner, and Romeo's self-scrutinies are over. The balcony-scene is like the singing of two birds; and its technical achievement lies in the sustaining at such length—with no story to tell, nor enlivening clash of character—of those simple antiphonies of joy.

Rosaline's adorer, aping disillusioned age, is hardly to be recognized in the boyishly, childishly happy Romeo that rushes to the Friar's cell. From there he goes to encounter Mercutio, still overflowing with spirits, apt for a bout of nonsense, victorious in it, too. From this and the meeting with the Nurse, back to the cell, to Juliet and the joining of their hands!

Note that the marriage and its consummation are quite simply thought of as one, by them and by the Friar. And fate accepts Romeo's challenge betimes.

> Do thou but close our hands with holy words,
> Then love devouring death do what he dare,
> It is enough I may but call her mine.

It is of the essence of the tragedy that, for all their passionate haste, the blow should fall upon their happiness before it is complete, that they must consummate their marriage in sorrow. And, in a sense, it is Romeo's ecstatic happiness that helps precipitate the blow. It lets him ignore Tybalt's insult:

> O sweet Juliet,
> Thy beauty hath made me effeminate,
> And in my temper softened valour's steel.

But, for all that, it has fired him to such manliness that he cannot endure the shame put upon him by Mercutio's death. Nothing is left now of the young Romeo, lovesick for Rosaline, and so disdainful of the family feud. His sudden hardihood is the complement to his chaffing high spirits of a few hours earlier; even as the grim

> This day's black fate on more days doth depend;
> This but begins the woe others must end.

makes a counterpart to his confident challenge to fate to give him Juliet and do its worst after. He must seem of a higher stature as he stands over Tybalt's body, stern, fated and passive to the next Capulet sword that offers, did not Benvolio force him away.

The hysterics of the next scene with the Friar, when he hears of his banishment, may seem as retrograde in character as they certainly are in dramatic method; but Shakespeare has taken the episode almost intact—and at one point all but word for word—from Brooke. And it does attune us, as we noted, to the fortuitous disasters of the story. Then the tragic parting of the two echoes the happy wooing of the first balcony-scene; and later in Mantua we find Shakespeare's Romeo, come to his full height.

Euphuism has all but vanished from the writing now. We have instead the dynamic phrase that can convey so much more than its plain meaning, can sum up in simplicity a ferment of emotion and thought.

> Is it even so? Then I defy you, stars!

is his stark comment on the news of Juliet's death; but what could be more eloquent of the spirit struck dead by it? He knows in a flash what he means to do. We are not told; Balthasar is to hire horses, that is all. Then, when he is alone:

> Well, Juliet, I will lie with thee to-night.

And what better epitome of the love in death, which is all that is left them![33]

There follows the scene with the apothecary; its skeleton Brooke's, its clothing Shakespeare's who employs it, not so much for the story's sake, as to give us, in repose, a picture of the Romeo his imagination has matured.

> How oft, when men are at the point of death,
> Have they been merry! which their keepers call
> A lightning before death. . . .

he lets him say later. He does not make him merry; but he gives him here that strange sharp clarity of eye and mind which comes to a doomed man, a regard for little things when his own end means little to him. He brings him to a view of life far removed from that first boyish, selfish petulance, to a scornful contemplation of what men come to, who will not dare to throw with fate for happiness, and be content to lose rather than be denied. As he watches the apothecary fumble for the forbidden poison:

> Art thou so bare, and full of wretchedness,
> And fearest to die? . . .

But for him it is:

> Come, cordial and not poison, go with me
> To Juliet's grave, for there must I use thee.

Life has broken him, and he in turn breaks all compact with life. If Balthasar dares to spy into the tomb his blood be on his head. He knows that he sins in killing himself: very well, he will sin. He implores Paris not to provoke him; but, provoked, he slaughters him savagely. At last he is alone with his dead.

At this juncture we lose much by our illegitimate knowledge of the story's end, and the actor of Romeo, presuming on it, usually makes matters worse. He apostrophizes Paris and Tybalt and Juliet at his leisure. But the dramatic effect here lies in the chance that at any minute, as we legitimately know, Juliet may wake or Friar Laurence come; and it is Romeo's haste—of a piece with the rest of his rashness—which precipitates the final tragedy. Shakespeare has provided, in the speech to the dead Juliet, just enough delay to stimulate suspense, but it must appear only as the last convulsive checking of a headlong purpose. He has added a last touch of bitter irony in letting Romeo guess at the truth that would have saved him, and her, and never guess that he guesses it.

> O my love! my wife!
> Death, that hath sucked the honey of thy breath,
> Hath had no power yet upon thy beauty:
> Thou art not conquered; beauty's ensign yet
> Is crimson in thy lips and in thy cheeks,
> And death's pale flag is not advanced there. . . .

After his glance at the dead Tybalt he turns to her again, obscurely marvelling:

> Ah, dear Juliet,
> Why art thou yet so fair? . . .

And it is upon a sardonic echo of the eloquence to which his love's first happiness lifted him that he ends. Then it was

> I am no pilot, yet, wert thou as far
> As that far shore washed by the farthest sea,
> I would adventure for such merchandise.

Now, the phial in his hand, it is

> Thou desperate pilot, now at once run on
> The dashing rocks thy sea-sick weary bark!
> Here's to my love! . . .

With that he drinks and dies.

From the beginning so clearly imagined, passionately realized in the writing, deeply felt at the end; this Romeo, when he had achieved him, must have stood to Shakespeare as an assurance that he could now mould a tragic figure strong enough to carry a whole play whenever he might want to.

JULIET

The first thing to mark about Juliet, for everything else depends on it, is that she is, to our thinking, a child.

Whether she is Shakespeare's fourteen or Brooke's six-teen makes little difference; she is meant to be just about as young as she can be; and her actual age is trebly stressed.[34] Her tragedy is a child's tragedy; half its poignancy would be gone otherwise. Her bold innocence is a child's, her simple trust in her nurse; her passionate rage at the news of Tybalt's death is easily pardonable in a child, her terrors when she takes the potion are doubly dreadful as childish terrors. The cant saying that no actress can play Juliet till she is too old to look her should therefore go the way of all parroted nonsense. A Juliet must have both the look and the spirit of a girl of from fourteen to sixteen, and any further sophistica-tion—or, worse, a mature assumption of innocence—will be the part's ruin. One must not compare her, either, to the modern girl approaching independence, knowing enough to think she knows more, ready to disbelieve half she is told. Life to Juliet, as she glimpsed it around her, was half jungle in its savagery, half fairy tale; and its rarer gifts were fever to the blood. A most precocious young woman from our point of view, no doubt; but the narrower and intenser life of her time ripened emotion early.

Not that there is anything of the budding sensualist in her; for to be sensual is to be sluggish, not fevered. Her passion for Romeo is ruled by imagination. And were this not the true reading of it, Shakespeare would have been all but compelled, one may say, to make it so; doubly compelled. Of what avail else would be his poetry, and through what other medium could a boy-ac-tress realize the part? The beauty of the girl's story, and its agonies too, have imagination for their fount. The height of her joy (anticipated, never realized) is reached in the imaginative ecstasy of

Gallop apace, you fiery-footed steeds. . . .

And she suffers to the full, even in thinking of them, all the shame of the marriage to Paris and the terrors of the vault.

Her quick florescence into womanhood is the more vivid for its quiet prelude; for the obedient

> Madam, I am here.
> What is your will?

when she first appears, for the listening to the Nurse's chatter, the borrowed dignity with which she caps her mother's snub that ends it, the simple

> It is an honour that I dream not of.

with which she responds to the hint of the great match awaiting her, the listening to her mother's talk of it and the

> I'll look to like, if looking liking move;
> But no more deep will I endart mine eye
> Than your consent gives strength to make it fly.

that seal our first impression of her. Where could one find a more biddable young lady?

What could one guess, either, from her first meeting with Romeo, from the demure game of equivoque she plays; though something shows, perhaps, in the little thrust of wit—

> You kiss by the book.

—by which she evades the confession of a kiss returned.[35] One moment later, though, there comes the first flash of the true Juliet; a revelation to herself, is it, as to us?

> My only love sprung from my only hate! . . .

And she stands, lost in amazement at this miracle that has been worked in her (even as Romeo will stand later lost in the horror of Tybalt's slaying), till the puzzled Nurse coaxes her away.

We next see her at her window. Yet again Shakespeare holds her silent a little, but for that one 'Ay me!' to tell us that now the still depths in her are brimming; when they brim over, again it is to herself she speaks.[36] The scene is conventionalized to a degree, with its overheard soliloquies, its conceits, its lyric flow. It turns every exigency of stage and acting to account, and its very setting, which keeps the lovers apart, stimulates passionate expression and helps sustain it. It left the boy-actress in imaginative freedom; nothing asked of him that his skill could not give. But the conceits come to life and blend insensibly with the simplicities. The fanciful

> Thou know'st the mask of night is on my face,
> Else would a maiden blush bepaint my cheek. . . .

flows into the frank coquetry of

> O gentle Romeo,
> If thou dost love, pronounce it faithfully;
> Or if thou think'st I am too quickly won,
> I'll frown and be perverse and say thee nay,
> So thou wilt woo; but else, not for the world.

and

> My bounty is as boundless as the sea,
> My love as deep; the more I give to thee,
> The more I have, for both are infinite.

comes from her as naturally as the very practical

> Three words, dear Romeo, and good-night indeed.
> If that thy bent of love be honourable,
> Thy purpose marriage, send me word to-morrow. . . .

And the scene's finest moment comes with

JULIET. Romeo!

ROMEO.   My dear?

JULIET.   At what o'clock to-morrow
 Shall I send to thee?

ROMEO.   By the hour of nine.

JULIET. I will not fail. 'Tis twenty years till then.
 I have forgot why I did call thee back.

ROMEO. Let me stand here till thou remember it.

JULIET. I shall forget, to have thee still stand there,
 Remembering how I love thy company.

ROMEO. And I'll still stay, to have thee still forget,
 Forgetting any other home but this.

This is the commonplace made marvellous. What is it, indeed, but the well-worn comic theme of the lovers that cannot once for all say goodbye and part turned to pure beauty by the alchemy of the poet? Modesty, boldness, shyness, passion, chase their way through the girl's speech; and Romeo, himself all surrender, sings to her tune. Together, but still apart, this is their one hour of happiness, and she is enskied in it, even as he sees her there.

We find her next, two scenes later, impatient for the Nurse's return with news of him; and in reckless delight and quick imagery for its expression she rivals Romeo now—the Juliet that could stand so mute! Then comes the quiet moment of the marriage. Making her reverence to the Friar, she may seem still to be the self-contained young lady we first saw; but even in the few lines of formal speech we hear a stronger pulse-beat and a deeper tone. She stands, not timidly at all, but just a little awed upon the threshold of her womanhood.[37]

After the tragic interval that sees Mercutio and Tybalt killed we find her alone again, and again her newly franchised self, expectant of happiness, the blow that is to kill it pending. To the modern Juliet, as we have noted, this scene probably presents more difficulties than any other in the play. Victorian Juliets customarily had theirs drastically eased by the eliminating of

> Gallop apace, you fiery-footed steeds. . . .

(some of the finest verse in the play) on the ground—God save the mark!—of its immodesty. One hopes that the last has been heard of such nonsense. But few performances since Shakespeare's time can have given the rest of the scene, with its elaborately embroidered rhetoric intact.[38] It will all of it, needless to say, be out of place upon a realistic stage; acted by a mature, ultra-feminine Juliet it will be intolerable. But we can hardly blame Shakespeare for that. He took here full advantage of his theatre's convention. The epithalamium has no more realism about it than a song or a sonnet would have; and the verbal embroideries which follow, meant to be taken at a high pitch of emotion and at a surprising pace, owe their existence in great part to the bravura skill of the boy-actresses who could compass such things with credit. The actress of today need not lack the skill, though the audiences may (and no great harm done) less consciously admire it; they probably will not break into applause as audiences at an opera do, as do French audiences at the declaiming of a fine passage of verse. She must think of the scene largely in terms of virtuosity; but there is far more in it, of course. It brings us the first clash of Montague and Capulet in other and sharper terms than swordplay, in the heart agonies of this child, as she is torn, now one way, now the other:

NURSE. Will you speak well of him that kill'd your cousin?
JULIET. Shall I speak ill of him that is my husband?

The tragedy is summed up for the first time in that.

Till now, we have seen Juliet at intervals; but with Romeo's farewell to her and his passing to Mantua she becomes for a space the sole centre of the play, while misfortune batters at her. In her helpless courage is the pathos, in her resolve from the first to kill herself sooner than yield—she is fourteen!—is the high heroism of the struggle. She is a child in the world's ways still. But she faces her mother when the marriage to Paris is broached, dignified and determined—and takes that good lady very much aback. The next moment, though, she has broken into a storm of impotent tears, which puzzle her father, but move him not at all, except to match and outdo her in storming. Her mother repulses her, her nurse betrays her; the trap is closing on her. She flies to the Friar. There is Paris himself; and for appearance' sake she must stop and parley with him while he claims her with calm assurance as his wife, must let him kiss her, even! Back she flies again from the shaken old man, armed with the only aid he can give her, one little less desperate than the dagger that never leaves her. The time is so short; and, in her distraction—playing the hypocrite as she must, and over-playing it—she even contrives to make it shorter. It escapes her quite that she will now—and fatally—not be following the Friar's directions.[39] She easily hoodwinks her mother and her nurse; then, left alone, outfacing terror, she drinks the potion.

She wakes in the vault, hopefully, happily:

> O comfortable friar, where is my lord?
> I do remember well where I should be,
> And there I am. Where is my Romeo?

to have for all answer,

> Thy husband in thy bosom there lies dead.

and to see Friar Laurence—even he!—turn and desert her. Should we wonder at the scorn sounded in that

> Go, get thee hence, for I will not away.

Romeo's dagger is all she has left.

The simplest reason for Juliet's leave-taking of life being short is that Romeo's has been long. But, theatrical effect apart, the sudden brutal blow by which her childish faith in the 'comfortable Friar' is shattered, and her unquestioning choice of death, make a fitting end to the desperate confidence of her rush to escape from what is worse than death to her. In the unreflecting haste of it all lies her peculiar tragedy. One day a child, and the next a woman! But she has not grown older as Romeo has, nor risen to an impersonal dignity of sorrow. Shakespeare's women do not, for obvious reasons, so develop. They are vehicles of life, not of philosophy. Here is a life cut short in its brightness; and it is a cruel business, this slaughter of a child betrayed.

88

Notes

1 In the Preface to *The Merchant of Venice* this discussion is raised again, and, of course, pursued at length in *Othello*.

2 The young gentlemen are gate-crashers, we perceive; there are few novelties in the social world! But Capulet is delighted; he even, when the unlooked-for fun is over and the recalcitrant regular guests have been coaxed to dance, presses a 'trifling foolish banquet' upon the strangers; cake and wine upon the sideboard, that is to say, and not, as the word now implies, a substantial sit-down affair. But etiquette, it seems, is against this. Having measured them a measure and so wound up the occasion very merrily, the 'strangers' do begone. Seriously, the conduct of this scene, when it is staged, needs attention. It is generally quite misunderstood and misinterpreted.

3 The company, that is to say, drift up towards the inner stage, from which, as from the withdrawing rooms beyond the great hall, Capulet and the guests had come to welcome the masked invasion, and as they all move away the guessing at who the strangers are dies down.

4 But for more argument about the question of act-division that is involved, see p. 57 ff.

5 The Bodleian has recently recovered its original First Folio, and the pages of the balcony-scene are the best thumbed of all.

6 Rowe is responsible for this. A few of the later editors scented something wrong, but only half-heartedly tried to put it right. Grant White was an honourable exception; but he places Mercutio and Benvolio in the orchard too. Juliet's line

The orchard walls are high and hard to climb. . . .

discounts that.

7 The effect will, of course, be intensified if he never leaves our sight, but the mere continuity of the scene, and our sense of him there, produces it.

8 One cannot too strongly insist upon the effect Shakespeare gains by this vivid contrast between scene and scene, swiftly succeeding each other. It is his chief technical resource.

9 He had been forced to a bout himself with Tybalt the day
before; and his description a little later of Romeo,

With gentle breath, calm look, knees humbly bowed...

has exasperation, as well, perhaps, as some politic exaggeration in it.

10 The slaughtering of Paris is wanton and serves little dramatic
purpose. Lady Montague is dead also by the end of the play
(though no one gives much heed to that) and Q1 even informs
us that

young Benvolio is deceased too.

Here, however, the slaughter is probably less arbitrary—from
one point of view. The actors had other parts to play. By the
time Q2 has come into being Shakespeare knows better than
to call attention to Benvolio's absence. Who notices it? But
his audiences—a proportion of them—no doubt loved a
holocaust for its own sake, and he was not above indulging
them now and then.

11 I say deliberately 'in all but one', not two, for the reason I
give later.

12 But we must do this throughout.

13 And we may rely on this as one of the very few authenticated
pieces of Shakespearean 'business'. For Q1 says,

Paris offers to goe in and Capolet calls him againe.

If the presumed reporter watching the performance thought
it important and had the time to note this down, it must have
been markedly done.

14 The musicians at Capulet's supper would probably have sat
in it; but this is hardly a dramatic use. Nor does the mere
association with Juliet *localize* it. There is no such scientific
precision in the matter.

15 For the stage business involved here, see p. 61 ff.

16 To Shakespeare's audience it would make little matter which
sort of curtains they were. A closed bed standing shadowed
on the inner stage is at once to be ignored and recognized.
We also, with a little practice, can ignore it, with Capulet;

though to our more privileged gaze there it significantly is, in suspended animation, as it were, till the Nurse, fingering its curtains, brings it back to dramatic life, as we have known she must, as we have been waiting breathlessly for her to do. Whether they should be bed curtains or stage curtains is a matter of convention, a question of more imagination or less.

17 We need not comb the text for objections to this arrangement, which is practicable, while no other is. For an explanation of

> Why I *descend* into this bed of death . . .

for instance, we have only to turn to Brooke's poem (lines 2620–2630). The frontispiece to Rowe's edition of the play is (incidentally) worth observing. It does not show a stage-setting, even a Restoration stage-setting, but the tomb itself may well be the sort of thing that was used. Paris and Romeo, it can be seen, wear semi-Roman costume. Is this, by any hazardous chance, explicable by the fact that Otway's perversion of the play, *Caius Marius*, was then current in the theatres (*Romeo and Juliet* itself was not, it seems, revived till 1744; and then much altered)? Did Du Guernier begin his drawing with the Roman lovers in his mind?

18 For no compelling reason; but Shakespeare felt the need of striking this note at once, since a first note will tend to be the dominant one.

19 Another instance of Shakespeare's use of time for momentary effect—or of his carelessness. Or will someone find a subtle stroke of character in the Watchman's inaccuracy?

20 It is of some interest to note that *Antony and Cleopatra* ends with a similar stage effect.

21 It looks as if another stool were needed on the outer stage when the Nurse returns to Juliet with her news of Romeo. But in this case no special provision is made either for its placing or removing.

22 The scene could have been staged in no other way. *Enter Romeo and Juliet at the window*, says Q1; *Enter Romeo and Juliet aloft*, says Q2. Later Q1 tells us, *He goeth downe*; and later still we have

> *Enter Nurse hastily.*

NURSE. Madame, beware, take heed the day is broke,
Your Mother's comming to your Chamber. Make all sure.
She goeth downe from the window.

  Whether Juliet or the Nurse, does not matter. In fact they
both must go down; for there follows immediately:

Enter Juliet, Mother, Nurse.

And a second later, after her

How now, who calls?

Juliet is on the stage. By Q2 the scene has been much
rewritten. The Nurse is given more time for her descent. The
later stage directions are less explicit. But that the business
was approximately the same is certain, if for no other reason
than that the last part of the scene, containing Capulet's
outburst, could have been effectively played nowhere but on
the lower stage.

23 'Or/and', as the lawyers sometimes have it, with regard to
the last possibility.

24 A casual phrase, surely, which means nearer two hours than
either one or three.

25 According to Q1 they were fiddlers, *i.e.* a consort of viols, so
they could not enter playing. Also, viols would not be well
heard through dialogue except from the musicians' gallery,
so their entrance was perhaps delayed by the time it took
them to finish there and descend. Q2 has the first reference
to 'pipes'. (Had the Globe acquired another quartet in the
meantime?) These could easily be heard playing 'off'. Q2,
however, marks no entrance for them. They are there when
the mourners depart; that is all. The entrance with Paris and
the Friar belongs to the undated Quarto, which is of doubtful
authority.

26 But this scene was badly muddled, either by the reporter of
these performances, or the actors, or by somebody. For
further discussion of the point, see note 37.

27 In her speech to Juliet 'a' mother has been read for 'your'
mother; but without any warrant.

28 Unless it be for Juliet's youthful, ruthless

Ancient damnation! O most wicked fiend! . . .

29 But *not* (to compare his position to Capulet's in Verona) of an English nobleman; of a prosperous English merchant, rather. See Miss St Clare Byrne's chapter on 'The Social Background' in *A Companion to Shakespearean Studies*.

30 We are not definitely told so, but certainly Mercutio seems a little the older of the two; and here again he is exempt from that other party-division into young and old.

31 All the technical talk of swordplay must, of course, have been a dozen times livelier to the Elizabethans than it ever can be to us.

32 Elizabethan kisses were given and taken with greater freedom and publicity and less significance than Victorian kisses, at any rate, were. But was not the kiss of greeting (which Erasmus found so pleasant) oftenest a kiss on the cheek? Romeo kisses Juliet on the lips.

33 This whole passage is also notable in that it calls for sheer acting, for the expression of emotion without the aid of rhetoric. This demand was a comparatively new thing when the play was written. Its fulfilment will have been one of the factors in the great success won.

34 It has been held that Shakespeare may have taken her age from a later edition of Brooke's poem in which the XVI had perhaps been transformed by the printer into XIV; also that he may have reduced her age to suit the very youthful appearance of some boy-actress. This is at any rate unlikely; fourteen is not distinguishable from sixteen on the stage. Moreover, he has other almost as youthful heroines: Miranda is fifteen, Perdita sixteen.

35 And how admirably suited to the effective resources of the boy-actress the pretty formality of this passage is!

36 Not a sigh, this! There is nothing sentimental about Juliet.

37 I make no attempt to say how and why this scene as it is in Q1 is so completely changed in Q2. But it is worth while remarking that we have far more than a rewriting of the words.

Enter Juliet somewhat fast and embraceth Romeo.

says Q1; and her first word is 'Romeo'. In Q2, on the contrary, it is

> Good even to my ghostly confessor.

and there is no sure sign that she embraces Romeo at all. I think myself that she does not, that the short scene was kept formal and dignified, the lovers standing on either side the Friar as if they were already before the altar.

38 For whatever reason, much of this is missing from Q1.

39 'Tomorrow night' she was to take the potion; but the wedding is suddenly put forward by a day. Juliet does not seem to notice what this may involve, and we may not either. Quite possibly Shakespeare didn't. At any rate he makes no use of the mistake, but brings in Friar John's mishap instead. The immediate effect of the extra haste was all he cared about.

Notes